# T. S. ELIOT
## A BIBLIOGRAPHY

# T. S. ELIOT

## A BIBLIOGRAPHY

INCLUDING CONTRIBUTIONS TO PERIODICALS

AND FOREIGN TRANSLATIONS

*by*

### DONALD GALLUP

*Assistant Professor of Bibliography*
*and Fellow of Jonathan Edwards College*
*Yale University*

NEW YORK

HARCOURT, BRACE AND COMPANY

# TABLE OF CONTENTS

# INTRODUCTORY NOTE

THIS bibliography is a revision and extension of my *Bibliographical Check-List of the Writings of T. S. Eliot*, which was published in May 1947 by the Yale University Library.[1] In the section devoted to T. S. Eliot's own books,[2] both English and American first editions are described in some detail, but for books which contain merely contributions by him, I have described in detail only the actual first edition in book-form, with notes on their first publication in the other country. Later impressions and editions are generally ignored except where some particular significance attaches to them.

The descriptive method I have used is intended to provide the information ordinarily needed about twentieth-century books, in a form simple and brief enough to be easily understood. It is based upon the method adopted by the American Library Association and used in the cards printed and distributed in the United States by the Library of Congress. I have modified this system, which ignores blank (and certain other) leaves, in order to account for all leaves, whether those upon which some printing appears, or blanks, or end-papers. Blank *pages* (i.e. the blank versos or rectos of printed leaves) are not mentioned in collations because they can obviously be inferred.

The general rule is that when the unnumbered printed preliminary leaves in a volume count up to the first numbered leaf, these leaves are not specified in the collation. When they do not count up, they are specified, e.g. 1 blank leaf, 3 leaves, 9–29 pp., since here the *printed* preliminary material counts up to only six unnumbered pages. When the first numbered page is the verso of a leaf unnumbered on the recto, the number of the recto is supplied in brackets, e.g. 1 blank leaf, 3 leaves, [9]–29 pp., thus indicating that 10 is the first page-number. The collation '29 pp.' alone would mean that the preliminary material counts up to the first numbered page and that the text ends on a page numbered 29; in this example page [30], being blank, is not specified. The collation '29, [1] pp.', on the other hand, would mean either that the text actually ends on the unnumbered page [30], or that an

---

[1] This in its turn was an elaborated version of *A Catalogue of English and American First Editions of the Writings of T. S. Eliot Exhibited in the Yale University Library 22 February to 20 March 1937*, published in February 1937.

[2] Syllabuses and other minor leaflets and broadsides are listed in the Appendix.

imprint, index, or some other printed material not part of the text appears on that page. '29 pp., 1 leaf' would indicate that the text ends on p. 29 and that additional material not a continuation of the text appears on a final unnumbered leaf, either recto or verso alone or both being printed.

Rather than encumber the descriptions of books with notes on prior periodical publication of individual poems and essays, an index of titles has been prepared containing references to first periodical publication as well as to first, and in some cases subsequent appearance in book-form.

Descriptions are based upon copies of the books themselves and the notes upon information supplied by publishers and other authorities. Where a copy of the book has not been examined, the title is starred. Although completeness has been aimed at, some items of trivial significance have been omitted, e.g. autobiographical data supplied for Harvard Class Books, *Who's Who*, &c., composite reports and letters to the press where the extent of T. S. Eliot's contribution, if any, could not be determined.

Although most of the books and many of the periodicals are in my own library, I have depended particularly upon the invaluable collection founded by T. S. Eliot's brother, the late Henry Ware Eliot, Jr., at Eliot House, Harvard, and now deposited in the Houghton Library. I should like to record again my great indebtedness to Henry Eliot, during his lifetime, and to his widow Theresa Garrett Eliot for help and encouragement over the past sixteen years. Mr. T. S. Eliot himself has answered innumerable questions with great patience and kindness and has not only called to my attention but often sent me items of which I should otherwise not have known. To the various publishers of Mr. T. S. Eliot's work, particularly Messrs. Faber & Faber and Messrs. Harcourt Brace, I am deeply indebted. I owe to Mr. John Hayward a particular debt for his kindness in reading my manuscript and, by his suggestions and corrections, making it far less faulty than it would otherwise have been.

For calling my attention to items and omissions and for other assistance I am grateful also to James T. Babb, Robert J. Barry, Herbert Cahoon, John Carter, Captain and Mrs. Louis Henry Cohn, G. W. Cottrell, Jr., Earl Daniels, Angel Flores, Kimon Friar, Henry Fuller, Philip Hofer, Sho Kajima, E. McKnight Kauffer, George Kirgo, Cecil Lang, Leon M. Little, William H. McCarthy, Jr.,

## Introductory Note

Harry F. Marks, Czeslaw Milosz, Norman Holmes Pearson, Mark Reinsberg, Eisig Silberschlag, Grover Smith, Kristian Smidt, John L. Sweeney, David L. Randall, Mr. and Mrs. Bertram Rota, Miss Frances Steloff, Mr. René Wellek, Miss Marjorie Gray Wynne, Edmund Wilson, John Cook Wyllie, Henry Zylstra, Leo Hamalian; and to the staffs of the University Library at Yale, and the Eliot House and Houghton Libraries at Harvard.

D. G.

JONATHAN EDWARDS COLLEGE
YALE UNIVERSITY
*December* 1951

# A

---

BOOKS AND
PAMPHLETS BY
T. S. ELIOT

A1         PRUFROCK AND OTHER         1917
              OBSERVATIONS

*First edition:*

PRUFROCK | AND | OTHER OBSERVATIONS | BY | T. S.  .
ELIOT | THE EGOIST LTD | OAKLEY HOUSE, BLOOMS-
BURY STREET | LONDON | 1917

> 40 pp. 18 × 12 cm. 1*s.* Stiff buff paper wrappers lettered in black on front cover.
>
> 500 copies were published in June 1917. 'The Egoist Subscription Form', a slip measuring approximately 9 × 12½ cm., was loosely inserted in some copies. The price was raised gradually to 5*s.*, at which price the remaining copies were sold in 1920–1. This book was not published in the United States, but its contents were re-printed in *Poems by T. S. Eliot* (New York, Knopf, 1920), pp. 37–63.
>
> A copy in my possession, with dimensions 18½ × 12½ cm., carries the following autograph inscription on the half-title: '. . . . One of twenty-five numbered copies of which this is No. 3. Justification de tirage T. S. E.' Concerning this copy Mr. Eliot wrote me on September 8, 1938: 'I had completely forgotten that any numbered signed copies of *Prufrock and Other Observations* had been issued. . . . I am sorry that my memory is so defective that I cannot tell you whether there really were 24 other numbered copies, or whether that was just my fancy, but if, as you say, the copy in your possession differs slightly from the ordinary edition, I can only suppose there was such a set, though what became of the other copies I have not the remotest notion.'
>
> CONTENTS: The Love Song of J. Alfred Prufrock—Portrait of a Lady—Preludes—Rhapsody on a Windy Night—Morning at the Window—The Boston Evening Transcript—Aunt Helen—Cousin Nancy—Mr. Apollinax—Hysteria—Conversation galante—La Figlia che Piange.

A2              EZRA POUND              1917
          HIS METRIC AND POETRY

*First edition:*

EZRA POUND | HIS METRIC AND POETRY | NEW YORK
[*ornament*] ALFRED A. KNOPF [*ornament*] 1917

> 31 pp. front. (port.). 19½ × 13 cm. 35c. Red boards lettered in gold on front cover; end-papers. Plain buff dust-wrapper.
>
> Issued anonymously on November 12, 1917, in connexion with the publication, also by Knopf, of Pound's *Lustra* (1917). Concerning this book, Eliot writes in *The Cantos of Ezra Pound: Some*

*Testimonies* (New York, Farrar & Rinehart [1933]), p. 16: 'There was a time when it did not seem unfitting for me to write a pamphlet, *Ezra Pound, His Poetry And Metric* [*sic*] but Ezra was then known only to a few and I was so completely unknown that it seemed more decent that the pamphlet should appear anonymously.' Its authorship was made public in Knopf's *The Borzoi 1920* (New York, 1920), p. 112, where it is listed among other books published by this firm as by T. S. Eliot, but with the incorrect date, 1918. This book was not published in England, nor reprinted in the United States.

## A3 POEMS 1919

*First edition:*

POEMS | BY | T. S. ELIOT | Printed & published by L. & V. Woolf | at THE HOGARTH PRESS, Hogarth House, Richmond | 1919

1 blank leaf, [13] pp. $23\frac{1}{2} \times 15\frac{1}{2}$ cm. 2s. 6d. Batik paper wrappers, with white paper label on front cover printed in red or (later?) black; sewn.

About 200 copies were published on June 20, 1919. The first copies printed have a typographical error, 'capitaux' for 'chapitaux' in line 11, page [13], corrected in later copies. This book was not published in the United States, but its contents were reprinted in *Poems* (1920), pp. 24–28, 31–36, where the title of 'Le Spectateur' is changed to 'Le Directeur'.

CONTENTS: Sweeney among the Nightingales—The Hippopotamus—Mr. Eliot's Sunday Morning Service—Whispers of Immortality—Le Spectateur—Mélange Adultère de Tout—Lune de Miel.

## A4 ARA VOS PREC [1920]

*a. First edition:*

Ara Vus Prec | by | T. S. Eliot | [*device*] | [London] THE OVID PRESS

2 blank leaves, 54 pp., 1 leaf, 2 blank leaves. $29 \times 23$ cm. Black paper boards or (later) cloth, yellow cloth back, with white paper label on spine printed upward in black: Ara Vos Prec T. S. Eliot; black end-papers.

*Colophon* (p. [55]): This edition of 264 copies is the first book printed by John Rodker and was completed Dec: 10th. 1919. Of the edition:—10 copies unnumbered are for review. 4 copies on Japan vellum numbered 1–4 & not for sale. 30 signed copies numbered 5–34. 220 copies numbered 35–255. The initials & colophon by E. A. Wadsworth.

Published by John Rodker early in February 1920. The first copies issued (among them presentation copies sent out by the author on February 5) were bound in black boards with yellow cloth back and

# A. *Books and Pamphlets*

paper label. The error 'Vus' for 'Vos' in the title was discovered after all the sheets had been printed and was corrected only on the label. Concerning the title, Mr. Eliot wrote me on February 21, 1936: 'The correct title of the book is *Ara Vos Prec*. It only happened to be *Vus* on the title page because I don't know Provençal, and I was quoting from an Italian edition of Dante the editor of which apparently did not know Provençal either. It would seem that there is no such word as *Vus* in that language.'

Of the copies on vellum, No. 1 (presented to John Quinn) is bound in black morocco with tan morocco back, stamped on front and back covers with decorative design in blind, and on front cover with title in gold: Ara Vos Prec. Another copy of this issue is unnumbered but has a certificate signed by John Rodker on p. [10] and is bound in red pigskin stamped with decorative design in blind on back cover and in blind and gold on front cover, and with title in gold on front cover: Ara Vus Prec. Both copies have black endpapers. The signed copies have the author's signature below the number on p. [10], but in all other respects are identical with the unsigned copies. Of these latter, several of the earlier numbers were used as presentation copies, carry the author's initials on p. [10], and are bound in paper boards with cloth back. The frequency with which unnumbered copies appear would seem to indicate that more than the scheduled ten were so issued. In any case there is evidence in a letter from T. S. Eliot to Rodker (now in the Schwab Collection at the University of Virginia) that only three copies were actually sent out for review purposes.

CONTENTS: Gerontion—Burbank with a Baedeker: Bleistein with a Cigar—Sweeney among the Nightingales—Sweeney Erect—Mr. Eliot's Sunday Morning Service—Whispers of Immortality—The Hippopotamus—A Cooking Egg—Lune de Miel—Dans le Restaurant—Le Spectateur—Mélange Adultère de Tout—Ode—The Love Song of J. Alfred Prufrock—Portrait of a Lady—Preludes—Rhapsody on a Windy Night—Morning at the Window—Conversation galante—Aunt Helen—Cousin Nancy—Mr. Appolinax [*sic*]—The Boston Evening Transcript—La Figlia che Piange.

*b. First American edition* (1920):

POEMS | by T. S. ELIOT | [*device*] | NEW YORK | ALFRED · A · KNOPF | 1920

63 pp. 20 × 13½ cm. $1.25. Tan paper boards stamped in brown on front cover and downward on spine; end-papers. Yellow dust-wrapper printed in green or brown.

Published on February 18, 1920. Although the poems occur in different order, the contents are identical with those of *Ara Vos Prec*, with the exception that 'Hysteria' is substituted for 'Ode' and 'Le Spectateur' is printed as 'Le Directeur'.

## A5 THE SACRED WOOD [1920]

*a. First edition:*

THE SACRED WOOD | ESSAYS ON POETRY AND CRITICISM | BY | T. S. ELIOT | METHUEN & CO. LTD. | *36* ESSEX STREET W. C. | LONDON

xviii pp., 1 leaf, *155*, [1] pp. $17\frac{1}{2} \times 11$ cm. *6s.* Blue cloth stamped in blind on front cover and in gold on spine (type of 'Methuen' at foot of spine measures approximately 3 mm.—later $3\frac{1}{2}$ mm.); end-papers. Salmon dust-wrapper printed in black. Later copies have the dust-wrapper completely re-set and may be identified by the addition of the sub-title on the front cover and the listing of *What is the Kingdom of Heaven* in the advertisements on the back cover as in its sixth edition.

Published on November 4, 1920. *On verso of title-page*: First published in 1920. A later binding-up of the sheets, issued not earlier than January 1924, has eight pages of publisher's advertisements inserted after p. [156].

CONTENTS: Introduction—The Perfect Critic—Imperfect Critics: Swinburne as Critic. A Romantic Aristocrat. The Local Flavour. A Note on the American Critic. The French Intelligence—Tradition and the Individual Talent—The Possibility of a Poetic Drama—Euripides and Professor Murray—Rhetoric and Poetic Drama—Notes on the Blank Verse of Christopher Marlowe—Hamlet and his Problems—Ben Jonson—Philip Massinger—Swinburne as Poet—Blake—Dante.

*b. American issue (1921):*

THE SACRED WOOD | ESSAYS ON POETRY AND CRITI-CISM | BY | T. S. ELIOT | [*device*] | NEW YORK | ALFRED A. KNOPF | 1921

The English sheets for *365* copies were imported, supplied with a cancel half-title and title (verso blank; pp. [i–iv]), and published in February 1921. $2.50. Blue cloth stamped in blind on front cover and in gold on spine; end-papers.

*c. Second edition ([1928]):*

THE SACRED WOOD | ESSAYS ON POETRY AND CRITICISM | BY | T. S. ELIOT | [*device*] | METHUEN & CO. LTD. | *36* ESSEX STREET W. C. | LONDON

xix, 171, [1] pp. $19\frac{1}{2} \times 13\frac{1}{2}$ cm. Blue cloth stamped in gold on spine; end-papers.

## A. *Books and Pamphlets*

*On verso of title-page*: First published (F'cap 8vo) November 4, 1920. Second edition (Crown 8vo) 1928.

Contains 'Preface to the 1928 Edition', dated March 1928, and signed, T. S. E.: pp. vii–x. The rest of the contents agrees with the first edition.

### d. *American issue (1930)*:

THE SACRED WOOD | ESSAYS ON POETRY AND CRITICISM | BY | T. S. ELIOT | [*device*] | NEW YORK | ALFRED A. KNOPF INC. | 1930

The English second edition sheets for 500 copies were imported and supplied with a cancel half-title and title (pp. [i–iv]), and published in 1930. $2.50. Marbled paper boards with black buckram back stamped in gold; end-papers.

## A6      THE WASTE LAND      1922

### a. *First edition*:

THE WASTE LAND | BY | T. S. ELIOT | [*quotation in three lines*] | NEW YORK | BONI AND LIVERIGHT | 1922

1 blank leaf, 3 leaves, 9–64 pp. $19\frac{1}{2} \times 13$ cm. $1.50. Flexible or (later) stiff black cloth lettered in gold on front cover and on spine; end-papers. Salmon dust-wrapper printed in black; outer glacine wrapper.

*Colophon (p. [6])*: Of the one thousand copies printed of The Waste Land this volume is number. . . . [*The number is stamped in type approximately 5 mm. (later 2 mm.) high.*]

Published on December 15, 1922. The first copies printed have the word 'mountain' correctly spelled in line 339 (p. 41); in later copies the 'a' has dropped out. Approximately the first 500 copies bound have the flexible cloth binding and figures 5 mm. high in the colophon.

Concerning its publication, Ezra Pound wrote in the Gotham Book Mart's catalogue *We Moderns* (New York, 1940), p. 24: 'The bearing of this poem was not over-estimated, nevertheless the immediate reception of it even by second rate reviewers was due to the purely fortuitous publication of the notes, and not to the text itself. Liveright wanted a longer volume and the notes were the only available unpublished matter.' The notes were not included in the periodical appearances of the poem in *The Criterion* and *The Dial*.

CONTENTS: I. The Burial of the Dead.—II. A Game of Chess.—III. The Fire Sermon.—IV. Death by Water.—V. What the Thunder Said.—Notes.

*b. Second impression* ([*1923?*]):

THE WASTE LAND | BY | T. S. ELIOT | [*quotation in three lines*] | NEW YORK | BONI AND LIVERIGHT

The pagination, size, price, and binding agree with those of the later copies of the first edition.

*Colophon* (*p.* [6]): One thousand copies of the Second Edition of The Waste Land were printed of which this volume is number. . . . [*Number stamped in type 2 mm. high.*]

Published probably early in 1923. Although called 'Second Edition' in the colophon, this is actually a second impression from the same setting of type as the first edition, but with a different colophon. With the incorrect 'mount in' in line 339 (p. 41).

*c. First English edition* (*1923*):

THE | WASTE LAND | T. S. ELIOT | [*quotation in four lines*] | PRINTED AND PUBLISHED BY LEONARD | AND VIRGINIA WOOLF AT THE HOGARTH | PRESS HOGARTH HOUSE PARADISE ROAD | RICHMOND SURREY | 1923

35 pp., 1 leaf, 1 blank leaf. 23 × 15 cm. 4s. 6d. Blue marbled paper boards with white paper label on front cover printed in black; front end-paper (final blank leaf pasted down as back end-paper).

About 460 copies were published on September 12, 1923. The label was used, apparently simultaneously, in three states: (1) measuring approximately 4 × 6 cm., with a border of asterisks; (2) measuring approximately $6\frac{1}{2} \times 9\frac{1}{2}$ cm., with heavy single-line rule above and below the title; (3) measuring approximately $6\frac{1}{2} \times 10$ cm., without rules.

'Previous Publications' of the Hogarth Press: recto of leaf following p. [36].

## A7    HOMAGE TO JOHN DRYDEN    1924

*First edition:*

HOMAGE TO | JOHN DRYDEN | THREE ESSAYS ON POETRY OF THE | SEVENTEENTH CENTURY | T. S. ELIOT | PUB-LISHED BY LEONARD AND VIRGINIA WOOLF | AT THE HOGARTH PRESS, TAVISTOCK SQUARE | LONDON, W. C. I | 1924

1 blank leaf, 3 leaves, 9–46 pp., 1 blank leaf. $21\frac{1}{2} \times 14$ cm. (The Hogarth Essays, No. 4) 3s. 6d. Stiff off-white paper wrappers printed in black on front cover; end-papers.

About 2,000 copies were published on October 30, 1924. This

book was not published in the United States, but its contents were reprinted in *The Hogarth Essays* (Garden City, N.Y., Doubleday, Doran, 1928), pp. [195]–239, issued in an edition of one thousand copies on September 28, 1928, and in *T. S. Eliot Selected Essays 1917–1932* (New York, Harcourt, Brace [1932]), pp. 264–74, 241–63.

CONTENTS: Preface—John Dryden—The Metaphysical Poets—Andrew Marvell.

A8        POEMS 1909–1925        1925

*a. First edition, ordinary issue:*

POEMS | 1909–1925 | By T. S. ELIOT | FABER & GWYER LTD | LONDON [*device*] MCMXXV

1 blank leaf, 3 leaves, 5–98, [1] pp. $20 \times 13\frac{1}{2}$ cm. 7*s.* 6*d.* Blue cloth with white paper label printed in black on spine; end-papers. Cream dust-wrapper printed in blue.

1,460 copies were published on November 23, 1925.

CONTENTS: Prufrock and Other Observations (1917)—Poems (1920)—The Waste Land (1922)—The Hollow Men (1925).

*b. Signed issue (1925* [i.e. *1926*]):

$23\frac{1}{2} \times 15$ cm. 25*s.* White buckram stamped in blind on covers and in gold on spine; end-papers.

*Colophon* (*verso of first leaf*): This demy octavo edition on hand-made paper is limited to eighty-five copies numbered and signed by the author, of which seventy-five are for sale. This is Number . . . [*signed*] T. S. Eliot.

Published on January 6, 1926.

*c. First American edition* ([*1932*]):

POEMS | 1909–1925 | BY | T. S. ELIOT | HARCOURT, BRACE AND COMPANY | NEW YORK · CHICAGO

128 pp. $22\frac{1}{2} \times 15$ cm. $2.00. Blue cloth stamped in gold on spine; end-papers. Cream dust-wrapper printed in blue.

4,080 copies were published on September 15, 1932.

A9      JOURNEY OF THE MAGI      [1927]

*a. First edition, ordinary issue:*

JOURNEY | OF THE MAGI | BY T. S. ELIOT | [*design*] | DRAW-INGS BY E. McKNIGHT KAUFFER [London, Faber & Gwyer Ltd.]

cover-title, [4] pp. 1 col. illus. $18\frac{1}{2} \times 12$ cm. (The Ariel Poems,

No. 8). 1s. Yellow paper wrappers printed in black on front and back covers, folded over blanks; sewn.

5,000 copies were published on August 25, 1927. Copies remaining unsold were reissued in February 1938, in mauve paper envelopes printed in black.

*b. Limited issue:*

cover-title, 2 blank leaves, [6] pp., 1 blank leaf. 1 col. illus. $18\frac{1}{2} \times 12\frac{1}{2}$ cm. (The Ariel Poems, No. 8) 5s. Yellow paper boards printed in black on front cover; end-papers. Glacine dust-wrapper.

*Colophon* (*p.* [6]): This edition on Zanders' hand-made paper is limited to 350 copies This is No. . . .

Published on November 23, 1927.

*c. First American edition* (1927):

Journey of the Magi | BY T. S. ELIOT | * | NEW YORK | WILLIAM EDWIN RUDGE | 1927

1 blank leaf, [4] pp., 1 leaf. $18\frac{1}{2} \times 12\frac{1}{2}$ cm. Grey paper wrappers folded in French style; stapled.

*Colophon* (*p.* [5]): Twenty-seven copies printed at the Printing House of William Edwin Rudge, Mount Vernon, N. Y., December, 1927. Twelve copies only for sale.

This and the other seven titles in the first year's series of Ariel Poems were reprinted by Rudge in order to secure copyright in the United States.


A10     SHAKESPEARE AND THE     1927
STOICISM OF SENECA

*First edition:*

THE SHAKESPEARE ASSOCIATION | SHAKESPEARE AND THE | STOICISM OF SENECA | (An Address read before the Shakespeare Association | 18th March, 1927) | BY | T. S. ELIOT | LONDON | PUBLISHED FOR THE SHAKESPEARE ASSOCIATION | BY HUMPHREY MILFORD, OXFORD UNIVERSITY PRESS | AMEN HOUSE, WARWICK SQUARE, E. C. | 1927

cover-title, 17, [1] pp., 1 blank leaf. $24\frac{1}{2} \times 15\frac{1}{2}$ cm. 2s. Grey paper wrappers printed in black on front cover; sewn.

Published on September 22, 1927. The essay was not separately published in the United States, but it was reprinted in *Selected Essays* ([1932]) pp. 107–20.

**A11  A SONG FOR SIMEON  [1928]**

*a. First edition:*

A SONG FOR | SIMEON | BY T. S. ELIOT | DRAWING BY E. McKNIGHT KAUFFER [London, Faber & Gwyer Ltd.]

cover-title , [4] pp. 1 col. illus. 18½ × 12 cm. (The Ariel Poems, No. 16) *1s.* Blue paper wrappers, printed in black on front and back covers, folded over blanks; sewn.

3,500 copies were published on September 24, 1928. Copies remaining unsold were reissued in February 1938, in grey paper envelopes printed in red. The poem was not separately published in the United States, but it was reprinted in *Collected Poems 1909–1935* ([1936]), pp. 127–8.

*b. Signed edition (1928):*

A SONG FOR | SIMEON | BY T. S. ELIOT | DRAWING BY | E. McKNIGHT KAUFFER | LONDON: FABER & GWYER LTD | 1928

6 leaves, 2 blank leaves, incl. 1 col. plate. 22 × 14½ cm. (The Ariel Poems, No. 16) *7s. 6d.* White boards printed in gold on front cover; end-papers.

*Colophon (recto of first leaf):* This large-paper edition, printed on English hand-made paper, is limited to five hundred copies This is number . . . [*signed*] T. S. Eliot.

Published on October 24, 1928.

**A12  FOR LANCELOT ANDREWES  [1928]**

*a. First edition:*

FOR LANCELOT ANDREWES | ESSAYS ON STYLE AND ORDER | BY | T. S. ELIOT | [*quotation in six lines*] | LONDON | Faber & Gwyer

1 blank leaf, 3 leaves, ix–xi, 13–143 pp. 19½ × 13½ cm. *6s.* Blue cloth with tan paper label on spine printed in black and blue; end-papers. Tan dust-wrapper printed in black and blue.

1,500 copies were published on November 20, 1928. (A few proof copies in grey paper wrappers were made up for the publishers before publication; in these the text differs slightly from that of the published edition.) *On verso of title-page*: First published in MCMXXVIII. . . .

CONTENTS: Preface—Lancelot Andrewes—John Bramhall—Niccolo Machiavelli—Francis Herbert Bradley—Baudelaire in Our Time—Thomas Middleton—A Note on Richard Crashaw—The Humanism of Irving Babbitt.

*b. First American edition (1929):*

FOR | LANCELOT ANDREWES | [*short rule*] | ESSAYS ON STYLE
AND ORDER | BY | T. S. ELIOT | [*quotation in eight lines, partly
enclosed by asterisks*] | GARDEN CITY, N. Y. | 1929 | DOUBLEDAY,
DORAN | AND COMPANY, INC.

> 1 blank leaf, viii pp., 2 leaves, 3–159 pp., 2 blank leaves. 21 × 13 cm.
> $2.00. Purple-brown cloth stamped in silver on front cover and on
> spine; end-papers. Grey dust-wrapper printed in red and blue.
>    2,000 copies were published on April 5, 1929. *On verso of title-
> page*: First edition

## A13                    DANTE                    [1929]

*a. First edition, ordinary issue:*

DANTE | BY | T. S. ELIOT | [*quotation in four lines*] | LONDON |
FABER & FABER | 24 RUSSELL SQUARE

> 69 pp., 1 blank leaf. 19½ × 13½ cm. (The Poets on the Poets, No. 2)
> 3s. 6d. Grey paper boards printed in black on front cover and on
> spine; end-papers; top edges stained blue or green. Grey dust-
> wrapper (designed by Rex Whistler) printed in blue and black.
>    2,000 copies were published on September 27, 1929. *On verso of
> title-page*: First published in MCMXXIX. . . . This book was not
> published in the United States, but its contents were reprinted in
> *Selected Essays* ([1932]), pp. 199–237.

*b. Signed issue:*

> 21½ × 14 cm. (The Poets on the Poets, No. 2) 21s. Blue-green cloth
> lettered downward in gold on spine; end-papers; top edges gilt.
> Glacine dust-wrapper.
>    *Colophon* (*p.* [1]): This edition printed on English hand-made paper
> is limited to one hundred and twenty-five numbered copies   This is
> number . . . [*signed*] T. S. Eliot.
>    Published on September 27, 1929.

## A14                    ANIMULA                    ⌜1929]

*a. First edition:*

ANIMULA | Bʏ T. S. ELIOT | [*design*] | Wood Engravings by |
GERTRUDE HERMES [London, Faber & Faber Ltd.]

> cover-title, [3] pp. 1 col. illus. 18½ × 12 cm. (The Ariel Poems,
> No. 23) 1s. Yellow paper wrappers printed in black on front and
> back covers, folded over blanks; sewn.

3,000 copies were published on October 9, 1929. Copies remaining unsold were reissued in February 1938, in green paper envelopes printed in brown. The poem was not separately published in the United States, but it was reprinted in *Modern Things, edited by Parker Tyler* (New York, The Galleon Press [1934]), pp. 16–17, issued in September 1934, and in *Collected Poems* ([1936]), pp. 129–30.

*b. Signed edition (1929):*

T. S. Eliot | ANIMULA | Wood Engravings by | Gertrude Hermes | London: | Faber & Faber Ltd | 1929

1 blank leaf, 7 leaves, incl. 1 illus., 1 col. plate. 22 × 14½ cm. (The Ariel Poems, No. 23) 7s. 6d. Yellow paper boards stamped in brown on front cover; end-paper.
*Colophon (recto of first leaf):* This large-paper edition, printed on English hand-made paper, is limited to four hundred copies This is Number . . . [*signed*] T. S. Eliot
Published on October 28, 1929.

## A15     ASH-WEDNESDAY     1930

*a. First edition:*

ASH-WEDNESDAY | BY | T. S. ELIOT | NEW YORK | THE FOUNTAIN PRESS INC. | LONDON | FABER & FABER LTD. | 1930

1 blank leaf, 5 leaves, 13–28 pp., 2 blank leaves. 20½ × 15 cm. 31s. 6d. ($7.50). Blue cloth stamped in gold on front cover and downward on spine; end-papers. Cellophane dust-wrapper with white paper flaps. Brown cardboard case.
*Colophon (recto of first leaf):* This signed and first edition, printed at The Curwen Press in March 1930, is limited to six hundred numbered copies. Of these, two hundred are reserved for sale in Great Britain and four hundred for sale in the United States of America. This copy is number . . . [*signed*] T. S. Eliot.
Published on April 24, 1930. It was at first intended to issue the book in large quarto format, but this plan was abandoned in favour of the smaller size.

*b. First ordinary edition:*

ASH-WEDNESDAY | BY | T. S. ELIOT | LONDON | FABER & FABER LTD. | 1930

2 blank leaves, 21 pp., 1 blank leaf. 20 × 13 cm. 3s. 6d. Brown cloth

stamped in gold on front cover and downward on spine; end-papers. Green dust-wrapper printed in black and red.

2,000 copies were published on April 29, 1930. *On verso of title-page*: This edition first published in MCMXXX ...

*c. First American ordinary edition:*

ASH-WEDNESDAY | BY | T. S. ELIOT | NEW YORK : LONDON | G. P. PUTNAM'S SONS | The Knickerbocker Press | 1930

2 blank leaves, 4 leaves, 13–29 pp., 1 blank leaf. $20\frac{1}{2} \times 15\frac{1}{2}$ cm. $1.50. Black cloth stamped in yellow on front cover and downward on spine; peach end-papers. Glacine dust-wrapper.

2,000 copies were published on September 26, 1930. *On verso of title-page*: Published, Autumn, 1930  First American trade edition ...

## A16     ANABASIS A POEM     1930 ## BY ST.-J. PERSE

*a. First edition, first ordinary issue:*

ANABASIS | a poem by | ST.-J. PERSE | [*ornament*] | with a | Translation into English | by | T. S. ELIOT | LONDON | FABER & FABER LIMITED | 24 RUSSELL SQUARE | 1930

1 blank leaf, 2 leaves, 7–75 pp. $26 \times 17$ cm. 10*s*. 6*d*. Green cloth stamped in gold on front cover and downward on spine; end-papers. White dust-wrapper printed all–over in green, black and red.

1,650 copies were published on May 22, 1930.

The French text and the English translation are printed on opposite pages.

St. J. Perse is the pseudonym of Alexis St. Léger Léger.

*b. Signed issue:*

75 pp. $26 \times 17$ cm. 31*s*. 6*d*. Green cloth stamped in gold on front cover and downward on spine; end-papers. Cellophane dust-wrapper. Green cardboard case.

*Colophon* (*p*. [1]): This signed edition, printed on English hand-made paper, is limited to three hundred and fifty numbered copies. This copy is number ... [*signed*] T. S. Eliot

Published on May 22, 1930.

*c. Second ordinary issue* (*1930* [i.e. *1937*]):

1 blank leaf, 2 leaves, 7–75 pp. $23 \times 16$ cm. 5*s*. Green cloth lettered in gold downward on spine; end-papers. Green dust-wrapper printed in purple.

1,101 sets of unsold sheets of the first edition (ordinary issue) were cut down, bound, and issued on February 4, 1937.

## A. *Books and Pamphlets*

*d. Second edition (first American edition; 1938):*

ANABASIS | A poem by St.=J. Perse | WITH A TRANSLATION
INTO ENGLISH BY | T. S. ELIOT | 1938 | HARCOURT, BRACE
AND COMPANY, NEW YORK

> 1 blank leaf, 2 leaves, 7–75 pp., 2 blank leaves. 22 × 15 cm. $1.25.
> Black cloth lettered in gold on spine; end-papers. Grey dust-
> wrapper printed in red.
>     1,000 copies were published on March, 3 1938. *On verso of title-
> page*: first American edition
>     For this American edition, which was not published in Great
> Britain, T. S. Eliot revised and corrected his translation.

*e. Third edition, revised and corrected ([1949]):*

ANABASIS | A poem by St.-John Perse | translated by T. S. Eliot |
Harcourt, Brace and Company New York

> 109 pp., 1 blank leaf. 23½ × 18½ cm. $4.00. Grey cloth lettered in
> blind on front cover and downward in gold on spine; end-papers.
> White dust-wrapper printed in green.
>     3,000 copies were published on November 10, 1949. *On verso of
> title-page*: First American edition, 1938   Revised and corrected
> edition, 1949. (A few proof copies in yellow wrappers were made
> up for the publishers before publication.) This edition, further
> revised by the translator, was not published in Great Britain.
>     Contains 'Note to revised edition', by T. S. Eliot, pp. 13–14.

## A17               MARINA               [1930]

*a. First edition:*

Marina | By T. S. Eliot | [*design*] | Drawings by E. McKnight Kauffer
[London, Faber & Faber Ltd.]

> cover-title, 2 leaves, incl. 1 col. plate. 19 × 12 cm. (The Ariel
> Poems, No. 29) 1*s*. Blue paper wrappers printed in black on front
> and back covers, folded over blanks; sewn.
>     2,000 copies were published on September 25, 1930. (A few
> proof copies, in slightly variant blue paper wrappers, were made up
> for the publishers before publication. Six of these were distributed
> by E. McKnight Kauffer, each signed and inscribed to the effect
> that the words 'Datta-Dayadhvam Damyata' in the illustration—
> present in these proof copies—were deleted at the poet's request.
> There are slight textual variations in these proof copies from the
> published text.) The poem was not separately published in the
> United States, but it was reprinted in *The New Poetry, An Antho-
> logy of Twentieth-Century Verse in English; edited by Harriet Monroe*

## A. *Books and Pamphlets*

*. . . and Alice Corbin Henderson. New ed., rev. and enl. by H.M.* (New York, Macmillan, 1932), pp. 163–4, in September 1932; in *An 'Objectivists' Anthology, edited by Louis Zukofsky* (Le Beausset, Var, France, New York, To, Publishers, 1932), pp. [160]–161, and in *Collected Poems* ([1936]), pp. 131–2.

*b. Limited edition (1930):*

T. S. ELIOT | MARINA | With Drawings by | E. McKnight Kauffer | London | Faber and Faber Ltd | 1930

1 blank leaf, 7 leaves, 2 blank leaves, incl. 1 illus., 1 col. plate. 22 × 14½ cm. (The Ariel Poems, No. 29) 7s. 6d. Blue boards stamped in gold on front cover; end-paper. Glacine dust-wrapper.
   *Colophon (recto of first leaf)*: This large-paper edition, printed on English hand-made paper, is limited to four hundred copies  This is Number . . . [*signed*] T. S. Eliot.
   Published on October 6, 1930.

## A18     THOUGHTS AFTER LAMBETH [1931]

*First edition:*

THOUGHTS AFTER LAMBETH | BY | T. S. ELIOT | LONDON | FABER & FABER LIMITED | 24 RUSSELL SQUARE

32 pp. 20 × 13½ cm. (Criterion Miscellany, No. 30) 1s. Brown paper wrappers printed in blue on front and back covers, folded over white cardboard; sewn.
   3,000 copies were published on March 5, 1931. An additional 300 copies in grey cloth stamped in gold on front cover were published simultaneously at 2s. These have double end-papers and a glacine dust-wrapper. *On verso of title-page*: First published in February [*sic*] MCMXXXI. . . . The essay was not separately published in the United States, but it was reprinted in *Selected Essays* ([1932]), pp. 310–32.

## A19          TRIUMPHAL MARCH          [1931]

*a. First edition:*

TRIUMPHAL MARCH | BY T. S. ELIOT | [*design*] | DRAWINGS BY E. McKNIGHT KAUFFER [London, Faber & Faber Ltd.]

cover-title, [4] pp. 1 col. illus. 19 × 12 cm. (The Ariel Poems, No. 35) 1s. Grey paper wrappers printed in black on front and back covers, folded over blanks; sewn.
   2,000 copies were published on October 8, 1931. This poem was

not separately published in the United States, but it was reprinted in *Modern Things* (New York [1934]), pp. 14–15, and in *Collected Poems* ([1936]), pp. 157–9.

*b. Limited edition (1931):*

TRIUMPHAL MARCH | BY T. S. ELIOT | DRAWINGS BY | E. McKNIGHT KAUFFER | LONDON | FABER & FABER LTD | 1931

    1 blank leaf, 6 leaves, 1 blank leaf, incl. 1 illus., 1 col. plate. $22\frac{1}{2} \times 14$ cm. (The Ariel Poems, No. 35) 7*s*. 6*d*. Grey paper boards stamped in gold on front cover; end-paper.
    *Colophon (recto of first leaf)*: This large-paper edition, printed on English hand-made paper, is limited to three hundred copies  This is Number . . . [*signed*] T. S. Eliot.
    Published on October 29, 1931.

# A20  CHARLES WHIBLEY A MEMOIR 1931

*First edition:*

THE ENGLISH ASSOCIATION | Pamphlet No. 80 | Charles Whibley | A Memoir | By | T. S. ELIOT | [London, Humphrey Milford, Oxford University Press] December 1931

    13, [3] pp. $25 \times 15\frac{1}{2}$ cm. (English Association Pamphlet, No. 80) 2*s*. Grey paper printed in black; sewn.
    Distributed to members of the English Association during December 1931, and published on January 14, 1932. Between four and five thousand copies were printed. The essay was not separately published in the United States, but it was reprinted in *Selected Essays* ([1932]), pp. 403–15.
    'Essays and Studies': [3] pp. following p. 13.

# A21   SELECTED ESSAYS 1917–1932 [1932]

*a. First edition (English), ordinary issue:*

SELECTED ESSAYS | 1917–1932 | BY | T. S. ELIOT | LONDON | FABER AND FABER LIMITED | 24 RUSSELL SQUARE

    454 pp., 1 blank leaf. $23 \times 15\frac{1}{2}$ cm. 12*s*. 6*d*. Red cloth lettered in gold on spine; end-papers. Green dust-wrapper printed in black.
    3,000 copies were published on September 15, 1932. (A few proof copies in plain white paper wrappers were made up for the publishers; in these the text varies slightly from that of the published edition.) *On verso of title-page*: First published in MCMXXXII . . .

# A. *Books and Pamphlets*

Concerning the incorrect dates assigned to certain of the essays in the table of contents, the author wrote to me on December 30, 1948: 'I think the explanation is that I dated the essays entirely by guess-work when I prepared the volume in 1932, and never bothered to look up the exact dates of first periodical publication.' The dates are, with one exception, corrected in the second American edition (New York, 1950), but one new error, '(1928)' for '(1929)' for 'Second Thoughts about Humanism' is made. All the dates are correctly printed in the third English edition (London, 1951).

CONTENTS: Tradition and the Individual Talent (1917 [i.e. 1919]) —The Function of Criticism (1923)—'Rhetoric' and Poetic Drama (1919)—A Dialogue on Dramatic Poetry (1928)—Euripides and Professor Murray (1918 [i.e. 1920])—Seneca in Elizabethan Translation (1927)—Four Elizabethan Dramatists (1924)—Christopher Marlowe (1918 [i.e. 1919])—Shakespeare and the Stoicism of Seneca (1927)—Hamlet (1919)—Ben Jonson (1919)—Thomas Middleton (1927)—Thomas Heywood (1931)—Cyril Tourneur (1931 [i.e. 1930])—John Ford (1932)—Philip Massinger (1920)— Dante (1929)—The Metaphysical Poets (1921)—Andrew Marvell (1921)—John Dryden (1922 [i.e. 1921])—William Blake (1920) —Swinburne as Poet (1920)—Lancelot Andrewes (1926)—John Bramhall (1927)—Thoughts after Lambeth (1931)—Baudelaire (1930)—Arnold and Pater (1930)—Francis Herbert Bradley (1926 [i.e. 1927])—Marie Lloyd (1923)—Wilkie Collins and Dickens (1927)—The Humanism of Irving Babbitt (1927 [i.e. 1928])—Second Thoughts about Humanism (1929)—Charles Whibley (1931)

*b. Limited issue:*

23 × 16 cm. *52s. 6d.* Blue vellum lettered in gold on spine; end-papers. Cellophane dust-wrapper.

*Colophon* (*p.* [2]): This edition printed on English hand-made paper is limited to one hundred and fifteen numbered copies each copy being signed by the author and of this number one hundred copies only are for sale This is number . . . [*signed*] T. S. Eliot

Published on September 15, 1932.

*c. First edition* (*American*):

T. S. ELIOT | [*short thick-thin rule*] | Selected Essays | 1917–1932 | HARCOURT, BRACE AND COMPANY | NEW YORK

1 blank leaf, x, 415 pp., 2 blank leaves. 22½ × 15½ cm. $3.50. Blue cloth stamped in gold on spine; end-papers. Tan dust-wrapper printed in purple.

3,700 copies were published on September 15, 1932, the same day as the English edition. *On verso of title-page:* first edition

## A. *Books and Pamphlets*

*d. Second American edition* ([1950]):

T. S. ELIOT | SELECTED | ESSAYS | NEW EDITION | Harcourt, Brace and Company | New York

> 1 blank leaf, 5 leaves, xiii–xiv, 460 pp., 3 blank leaves. 22 × 15 cm. $4.50. Black cloth lettered in gold on spine; end-papers. Salmon dust-wrapper printed in green.
>
> 5,000 copies were published on October 5, 1950.
>
> Contains a note to the new edition, p. [ix]. This edition expands the original volume of *Selected Essays 1917–1932* by including four essays from *Essays Ancient and Modern*: 'In Memoriam (1936)', 'Religion and Literature (1935)', 'The *Pensées* of Pascal (1931)', and 'Modern Education and the Classics (1932)'.

*e. Third English edition* ([1951]):

SELECTED ESSAYS | BY | T. S. ELIOT | LONDON | FABER AND FABER LIMITED | 24 RUSSELL SQUARE

> 516 pp. 22½ × 15 cm. 20s. Brown cloth lettered in gold on spine; end-papers. Yellow dust-wrapper printed in black.
>
> 4,700 copies were published on September 3, 1951. *On verso of title-page*: First published in MCMXXXII . . . Second edition revised and enlarged October MCMXXXIV . . . Third enlarged edition April [*sic*] MCMLI . . .
>
> Contains (pp. 7–8) the same note as that printed in the second American edition described above, but with the date changed to April 1951. The second English edition (1934) reprinted the essay 'John Marston' from *Elizabethan Essays* (1934) but contained no other new material. This third English edition reprints the contents of the second English edition, and adds the same four essays from *Essays Ancient and Modern* reprinted in the second American edition.

A22     JOHN DRYDEN THE POET     1932
     THE DRAMATIST THE CRITIC

*a. First edition, ordinary issue:*

JOHN DRYDEN | THE POET | THE DRAMATIST | THE CRITIC | Three Essays by T. S. ELIOT | [*ornament in brown*] | NEW YORK | TERENCE & ELSA HOLLIDAY | 1932

> 2 blank leaves, 67, [1] pp. 20 × 14 cm. $1.50. Brown paper boards stamped with label in black and gold on front cover and on spine; end-papers. White dust-wrapper printed in brown.
>
> 1,000 copies were published on October 18, 1932.

# A. *Books and Pamphlets*

*b. Limited issue:*

4 leaves, [5]–67, [1] pp., incl. col. front. (port.) 20½ × 14 cm. $7.50. Marbled paper boards, with black cloth back lettered upward in gold on spine; end-papers. Cellophane dust-wrapper.

*Colophon (recto of first leaf)*: 110 copies of this special edition have been printed. 100 copies are for sale. no. . . . [*signed*] T. S. Eliot Published on October 18, 1932.

## A23     SWEENEY AGONISTES     [1932]

*First edition:*

SWEENEY AGONISTES | FRAGMENTS OF AN | ARISTO-PHANIC MELODRAMA | BY | T. S. ELIOT | LONDON | FABER & FABER LIMITED | 24 RUSSELL SQUARE

31 pp. 19 × 12½ cm. 2*s*. 6*d*. Blue or (later) blue-green paper boards lettered downward in red on spine; end-papers. Yellow dust-wrapper printed in blue.

4,100 copies were published on December 1, 1932. *On verso of title-page*: First published December MCMXXXII. . . . This book was not separately published in the United States, but its contents were reprinted in *Collected Poems* ([1936]), pp. 135–54.

CONTENTS: Fragment of a Prologue—Fragment of an Agon.

## A24     THE USE OF POETRY     [1933] AND THE USE OF CRITICISM

*a. First edition (English):*

THE USE OF POETRY | AND THE USE OF CRITICISM | STUDIES IN | THE RELATION OF CRITICISM | TO POETRY IN ENGLAND | BY | T. S. ELIOT | Charles Eliot Norton Professor of Poetry | in Harvard University | 1932–1933 | LONDON | FABER AND FABER LIMITED | 24 RUSSELL SQUARE

1 blank leaf, 3 leaves, 9–156 pp., 2 blank leaves. 23 × 15 cm. 7*s*. 6*d*. Red cloth lettered in gold on spine; end-papers. Blue dust-wrapper printed in black and red.

2,500 copies were published on November 2, 1933. *On verso of title-page*: First published November MCMXXXIII. . . .

CONTENTS: Prefatory Note—Introduction (November 4, 1932)—Apology for the Countess of Pembroke (November 25, 1932)—The Age of Dryden (December 2, 1932)—Wordsworth and Coleridge

(December 9, 1932)—Shelley and Keats (February 17, 1933)—
Matthew Arnold (March 3, 1933)—The Modern Mind (March 17,
1933)—Conclusion (March 31, 1933)

*b. First edition (American; 1933)* :

THE USE OF POETRY | AND THE USE OF CRITICISM |
STUDIES IN | THE RELATION OF CRITICISM | TO POETRY
IN ENGLAND | THE CHARLES ELIOT NORTON LECTURES
FOR 1932–1933 | BY | T. S. ELIOT | [*device*] | HARVARD UNIVER-
SITY PRESS | CAMBRIDGE, MASSACHUSETTS | 1933

viii pp., 2 leaves, [3]–149 pp. 21½ × 14½ cm. $2.00. Red cloth
stamped in blind on front and back covers and in gold on spine;
end-papers. Cream dust-wrapper printed in black and green.
Published on November 2, 1933, the same day as the English
edition.

## A25    AFTER STRANGE GODS    [1934]

*a. First edition:*

AFTER STRANGE GODS | A PRIMER | OF MODERN HERESY
| THE PAGE-BARBOUR LECTURES | AT THE UNIVERSITY
OF VIRGINIA | 1933 | BY | T. S. ELIOT | [*quotation in four lines*] |
LONDON | FABER AND FABER LIMITED | 24 RUSSELL
SQUARE

1 blank leaf, 4 leaves, 11–68 pp. 23 × 14½ cm. 3*s.* 6*d.* Black cloth
lettered downward in gold on spine; end-papers. Red dust-wrapper
printed in black and blue.
3,000 copies were published on February 22, 1934. *On verso of
title-page*: First published in February MCMXXXIV . . .

*b. First American edition:*

After Strange Gods | A PRIMER OF MODERN HERESY | BY |
T. S. ELIOT | THE PAGE-BARBOUR LECTURES | AT | THE
UNIVERSITY OF VIRGINIA | 1933 | [*quotation in four lines,
between two ornaments*] | HARCOURT, BRACE AND COMPANY |
NEW YORK

1 blank leaf, 72 pp., 3 blank leaves. 22½ × 15½ cm. $1.25. Red cloth
lettered downward in gold on spine; end-papers. Tan dust-wrapper
printed in black and red.
1,500 copies were published on April 19, 1934. *On verso of title-
page*: first edition

## A26 THE ROCK [1934]

*a. First edition:*

THE ROCK | A PAGEANT PLAY | WRITTEN FOR PERFORM-
ANCE | AT SADLER'S WELLS THEATRE | 28 MAY—9 JUNE
1934 | ON BEHALF OF THE | FORTY-FIVE CHURCHES FUND
| OF THE DIOCESE OF | LONDON | BOOK OF WORDS BY |
T. S. ELIOT | LONDON | FABER & FABER LIMITED | 24
RUSSELL SQUARE

1 blank leaf, 86 pp., 2 blank leaves. 19 × 12½ cm. 1*s*. Stiff grey paper
wrappers printed in black on front cover and on spine, folded over
blanks; sewn.

2,000 copies were published on May 31, 1934. Of these, 1,000
copies were already on sale at the Theatre beginning May 28. An
additional thousand copies in grey paper boards lettered downward
in blue on spine and with a white dust-wrapper printed in grey and
red were published simultaneously on May 31, at 2*s. 6d.* In these,
the blank leaves of the paper-bound copies have become end-papers.
*On verso of title-page*: First published in May MCMXXXIV. . . .
The Builders' Song, with the music by Martin Shaw, was issued
separately in the same year in London by Messrs. J. B. Cramer &
Co., Ltd., under the title, *The Builders Song from 'The Rock'.*

A slip concerning the Iconoclasm scene, measuring approximately 11 × 14½ cm., was loosely inserted in some copies.

*b. First American edition:*

THE ROCK | A PAGEANT PLAY, WRITTEN FOR PERFORM-
ANCE | AT SADLER'S WELLS THEATRE | 28 MAY–9 JUNE
1934 | ON BEHALF OF THE | FORTY-FIVE CHURCHES FUND
| OF THE DIOCESE OF LONDON | Book of Words by | T. S.
ELIOT | [*ornament*] | HARCOURT, BRACE AND COMPANY |
NEW YORK

1 blank leaf, 86 pp., 4 blank leaves. 19½ × 13 cm. $1.00. Tan cloth
with red paper label printed in black on spine; end-papers. White
dust-wrapper printed in grey and red.

1,500 copies were published on August 23, 1934. *On verso of
title-page*: first edition

## A27 ELIZABETHAN ESSAYS [1934]

*First edition:*

ELIZABETHAN | ESSAYS | BY | T. S. ELIOT | LONDON |
FABER & FABER LIMITED | 24 RUSSELL SQUARE

195 pp. 18½ × 12½ cm. (The Faber Library, No. 24) 3*s. 6d.* Green

cloth stamped in gold on spine; end-papers. Blue dust-wrapper printed in red and black.

4,000 copies were published on October 4, 1934. Only the last essay, 'John Marston', is printed here for the first time in book form; the others are reprinted from *Selected Essays* (1932). *On verso of title-page*: First published in October MCMXXXIV . . .

Early copies have a misprint in the series note on the half-title (p. [1]), 'No. 21' for 'No. 24'. Later copies have a cancel half-title, with the series note correctly printed.

CONTENTS: Four Elizabethan Dramatists—Christopher Marlowe —Shakespeare and the Stoicism of Seneca—Hamlet—Ben Jonson— Thomas Middleton—Thomas Heywood—Cyril Tourneur—John Ford—Philip Massinger—John Marston.

A28 WORDS FOR MUSIC [1935]

*First separate edition:*

WORDS | FOR | MUSIC | * | T. S. | ELIOT | 1934 [Bryn Mawr, Pennsylvania]

1 blank leaf, [4] pp., 1 blank leaf. $16\frac{1}{2} \times 11\frac{1}{2}$ cm. Paper wrappers with labels, as described below, folded over blanks; sewn.

*Colophon* (*p.* [4]): Twenty copies of Words for Music were printed for the author: six on Oxhead, numbered 1–6 [and bound in marbled paper wrappers with white paper label]; six on Leipzig, numbered I–VI [and bound in decorated paper wrappers with silver paper label]; six on Rives, numbered a–f [and bound in gold paper wrappers with white paper label]; and two on Imperial vellum, numbered A and B [and bound in red and gold paper wrappers with gold paper label and cellophane dust-wrapper with white paper label]. . . . Some copies were issued with a spare label tipped in at the end.

Printed for Frederic Prokosch at the 'Bryn Mawr Press', Bryn Mawr, Pennsylvania, for distribution by the author in February 1935. With various 'proof' and 'special' copies and those numbered in duplicate, the size of the printing was apparently substantially greater than the twenty copies indicated by the colophon.

Reprinted from *The Virginia Quarterly Review*, April 1934, and from *The Best Poems of 1934, selected by Thomas Moult* ([1934]), p. 107. For a fuller description of the latter see below B30.

CONTENTS: New Hampshire—Virginia.

A29 MURDER IN THE 1935
CATHEDRAL

*a. First (acting) edition:*

MURDER | IN THE | CATHEDRAL | by | T. S. ELIOT | Acting

# A. *Books and Pamphlets*

Edition | for the Festival of the Friends of Canterbury Cathedral | 1935 | Canterbury | H. J. GOULDEN, LIMITED | (by permission of the Author and Messrs. Faber and Faber)

> 1 blank leaf, 1 leaf, 38 pp., 1 blank leaf. $18\frac{1}{2} \times 12\frac{1}{2}$ cm. 1*s*. Stiff, pale lilac paper wrappers printed in purple on front cover. (A few copies, in stiff, plain white paper wrappers, were issued to members of the cast before the printed wrappers were ready.)
>
> 750 copies were published on May 10, 1935, for sale at performances of the play in Canterbury Cathedral. The text was slightly altered and abbreviated for the production and is so printed in this edition.

*b. First complete edition* ([*1935*]):

MURDER | IN THE CATHEDRAL | by | T. S. Eliot | London | Faber and Faber Limited | 24 Russell Square

> 1 blank leaf, 2 leaves, 7–87 pp., 4 blank leaves. $22\frac{1}{2} \times 14\frac{1}{2}$ cm. 5*s*. Purple cloth lettered downward in gold on spine; end-papers. Blue dust-wrapper printed in red and black.
>
> 3,000 copies were published on June 13, 1935. *On verso of title-page*: First published in June MCMXXXV . . .

*c. Second edition* ([*1936*]):

> 1 blank leaf, 2 leaves, 7–86 pp., 5 blank leaves. $22\frac{1}{2} \times 14\frac{1}{2}$ cm. 5*s*. Purple cloth lettered downward in gold on spine; end-papers. Blue dust-wrapper printed in red and black.
>
> Published in January 1936. 'In this second edition I have substituted, for the dialogue of the three Priests at the beginning of Part II, a speech by the Chorus. The text is now in conformity with the recent production at the Mercury Theatre, London'—*Author's note*, p. 7. *On verso of title-page*: First published in June MCMXXXV . . . Second edition January MCMXXXVI . . .

*d. Third edition* ([*1937*]):

> 1 blank leaf, 2 leaves, 7–91 pp., 2 blank leaves. $22\frac{1}{2} \times 14\frac{1}{2}$ cm. 5*s*. Purple cloth lettered downward in gold on spine; end-papers. Blue dust-wrapper printed in red and black.
>
> Published in August 1937. 'In the second editio . a chorus was substituted for the introits which, in the first edition, constituted the opening of Part II. To this third edition the introits have been added as an appendix, and may be used instead of that chorus in productions of the play. . . . I have in Part II reassigned most of the lines formerly attributed to the Fourth Knight. When, as was originally intended, the parts of the Tempters are doubled with those of the Knights, the advantage of these alterations should be obvious'—*Author's note*, p. 7. *On verso of title-page*: First published in June MCMXXXV . . . Third edition August MCMXXXVII . . .

# A. *Books and Pamphlets*

*e. Fourth (school) edition ([1938]):*

1 blank leaf, 2 leaves, 7–88 pp., 4 blank leaves. 20½ × 14 cm. *2s. 6d.* Grey cloth lettered downward in black on spine; end-papers.

'School edition', published in September 1938. 'In this fourth edition certain further rearrangements and deletions have been made, which have been found advisable by experiment in the course of production'—*Author's note*, p. 7. *On verso of title-page*: First published in this new edition September MCMXXXVIII . . .

*f. First American edition ([1935]):*

MURDER | in the Cathedral | BY T. S. ELIOT | HARCOURT, BRACE AND COMPANY | NEW YORK

1 blank leaf, 4 leaves, 11–87 pp., 2 blank leaves. 22½ × 15 cm. $1.25. Black cloth lettered downward in gold on spine; end-papers. White dust-wrapper printed in plum and black.

1,500 copies were published on September 19, 1935. *On verso of title-page*: first edition

*g. Second American edition ([1936]):*

1 blank leaf, 4 leaves, 11–86 pp., 1 blank leaf. 22½ × 15 cm. $1.25. Black cloth lettered downward in gold on spine; end-papers. White dust-wrapper printed in plum and black.

2,000 copies were published in June 1936 from the second (English) edition.

A30         TWO POEMS         1935

*First edition:*

TWO | POEMS | * | T. S. | ELIOT | CHRISTMAS | 1935 [Cambridge, Printed at the Cambridge University Press]

1 blank leaf, [4] pp., 1 blank leaf. 16½ × 11½ cm. Paper wrappers with labels as described below, folded over blanks; sewn.

*Colophon (p. [4]):* Twenty-two copies of these poems were printed for the author: five on Arches, numbered 1–5 [and bound in decorated paper wrappers, with grey paper label]; five on Normandie numbered I–V [and bound in yellow heavy paper wrappers, with silver label]; five on Bremen, numbered a–e [and bound in green paper wrappers, with grey paper label]; five on Brussels parchment, numbered A–E [and bound in marbled paper wrappers, with white paper label]; and two on red Florentine, numbered X and XX [and bound in silver paper wrappers, with red paper label]. . . . Some copies were issued with a spare label tipped in at the end.

Printed for Frederic Prokosch at the Cambridge University Press,

in October 1935, for distribution by the author at Christmas 1935. The poems were not separately published in the United States, but they were reprinted in *Collected Poems* ([1936]), pp. 175, 173.
CONTENTS: Cape Ann—Usk.

A31        ESSAYS        [1936]
## ANCIENT AND MODERN

*a. First edition:*

ESSAYS | ANCIENT & MODERN | by | T. S. ELIOT | London | FABER AND FABER LIMITED | 24 Russell Square

190 pp., 1 blank leaf. $19\frac{1}{2} \times 13$ cm. *6s.* Blue cloth lettered in gold on spine; end-papers. Green dust-wrapper printed in black and blue.

2,500 copies were published on March 5, 1936. (A few proof copies in blue paper wrappers were made up for the publishers before publication; in these the text differs slightly from that of the published edition.) *On verso of title-page*: First published in March Mcmxxxvi . . .

CONTENTS: Preface—Lancelot Andrewes—John Bramhall—Francis Herbert Bradley—Baudelaire in Our Time—The Humanism of Irving Babbitt—Religion and Literature—Catholicism and International Order—The *Pensées* of Pascal—Modern Education and the Classics—In Memoriam.

*b. First American edition:*

ESSAYS | ANCIENT AND MODERN | BY T. S. ELIOT | HARCOURT, BRACE AND COMPANY | NEW YORK

vii pp., 2 leaves, 3–203 pp., 1 blank leaf. $19\frac{1}{2} \times 13\frac{1}{2}$ cm. $2.00. Blue (later, darker blue) cloth lettered in gold on spine; end-papers. Grey dust-wrapper printed in red.

2,500 copies were published on August 27, 1936. *On verso of title-page*: first American edition

A32    COLLECTED POEMS 1909–1935 [1936]

*a. First edition:*

Collected Poems | 1909–1935 | by | T. S. Eliot | London | Faber & Faber Limited | 24 Russell Square

191 pp. $22\frac{1}{2} \times 15$ cm. *7s. 6d.* Blue cloth lettered in gold on spine; end-papers. Red dust-wrapper printed in blue and black.

6,000 copies were published on April 2, 1936. (A few proof copies in orange paper wrappers were made up for the publishers before publication; in these, text and typography differ slightly from those of the published edition.) *On verso of title-page*: First published in April Mcmxxxvi . . .

A selection from this book, with title *The Waste Land and Other Poems*, was published in February 1940, by Faber and Faber in their series 'Sesame Books'. The second half was reprinted separately in May 1941, with title *Later Poems 1925–1935*, as no. 50 in 'The Faber Library'. In July 1948, the major part of this book was reprinted by Penguin Books in an edition of 50,000 copies at 1*s.* 6*d.*, with title *Selected Poems*.

CONTENTS: Prufrock (1917)—Poems (1920)—The Waste Land (1922)—The Hollow Men (1925)—Ash-Wednesday (1930)—Ariel Poems—Unfinished Poems—Minor Poems—Choruses from 'The Rock'—Burnt Norton.

*b. First American edition:*

T. S. ELIOT | COLLECTED | POEMS | 1909–1935 | Harcourt, Brace and Company | New York

220 pp., 2 blank leaves. 22 × 15 cm. $2.50. Blue cloth lettered in gold on spine; end-papers. Grey or (later) brown dust-wrapper printed in red.

4,700 copies were published on May 21, 1936. *On verso of title-page*: First American Edition

## A33      THE FAMILY REUNION     [1939]

*a. First edition:*

THE | FAMILY REUNION | a play by | T. S. Eliot | Faber and Faber Limited | 24 Russell Square | London

1 blank leaf, 4 leaves, 11–136 pp. 22½ × 15 cm. 7*s.* 6*d.* Grey cloth lettered downward in red on spine; end-papers. Cream dust-wrapper printed in red, green, and black.

6,375 copies were published on March 21, 1939. (A few proof copies in yellow paper wrappers were made up for the publishers before publication.) *On verso of title-page*: First published in March MCMXXXIX . . .

*b. First American edition:*

The Family Reunion | A play by T. S. ELIOT | Harcourt, Brace and Company, New York

1 blank leaf, 4 leaves, 11–131 pp. 22 × 15 cm. $1.50. Black cloth lettered downward in gold on spine; end-papers. Yellow dust-wrapper printed in brown.

2,500 copies were published on March 30, 1939. *On verso of title-page*: first American edition

A34        OLD POSSUM'S       [1939]
BOOK OF PRACTICAL CATS

*a. First edition:*

T. S. ELIOT | [*rule*] | OLD POSSUM'S BOOK | OF PRACTICAL
CATS | FABER AND FABER LIMITED | 24 Russell Square |
London

> 1 blank leaf, 2 leaves, 7–45 pp., 1 blank leaf. 22½ × 17 cm. 3s. 6d.
> Yellow cloth printed in red on front cover and downward on spine;
> end-papers. Yellow dust-wrapper printed in black with pictorial
> designs by the author.
>
> 3,005 copies were published on October 5, 1939. (A few proof
> copies in yellow paper wrappers were made up for the publishers
> before publication.) *On verso of title-page*: First published in September [*sic*] Mcmxxxix . . .
>
> CONTENTS: Preface—The Naming of Cats—The Old Gumbie Cat
> —Growltiger's Last Stand—The Rum Tum Tugger—The Song of
> the Jellicles—Mungojerrie and Rumpelteazer—Old Deuteronomy
> —The Pekes and the Pollicles—Mr. Mistoffelees—Macavity: The
> Mystery Cat—Gus: The Theatre Cat—Bustopher Jones: The Cat
> about Town—Skimbleshanks: The Railway Cat—The Ad-dressing
> of Cats.

*b. First American edition:*

T. S. ELIOT | [*line*] | OLD POSSUM'S | BOOK | OF | PRACTICAL |
CATS | [*illustration below and to right of above five lines*] | [New York]
HARCOURT, BRACE AND COMPANY

> 5 leaves, 9–46 pp., 1 blank leaf. 22 × 16 cm. $1.25. Grey cloth
> lettered downward in black on spine; end-papers. Orange dust-
> wrapper printed in black with pictorial designs by the author.
>
> The title-page, printed on orange paper with the author's
> pictorial designs, is inserted.
>
> 2,000 copies were published on November 16, 1939. *On verso of
> title-page*: first American edition

*c. Illustrated edition* ([1940]):

T. S. ELIOT | [*rule*] | OLD POSSUM'S BOOK | OF PRACTICAL
CATS | [*rule*] | NICOLAS BENTLEY | drew the pictures | [*design*] |
FABER AND FABER LIMITED | 24 Russell Square | London

> 1 blank leaf, 2 leaves, 7–50, [1] pp. illus., 14 col. plates. 22 × 16½ cm.
> 7s. 6d. Cream cloth stamped with coloured design on front cover
> and downward in red on spine; end-papers. Cream dust-wrapper
> printed with coloured pictorial design and in black and red.

Published in November 1940. *On verso of title-page*: First published in September Mcmxxxix . . . First illustrated edition November Mcmxl . . .

A35        THE IDEA OF A       [1939]
             CHRISTIAN SOCIETY

*a. First edition:*

THE IDEA OF A | CHRISTIAN SOCIETY | BY | T. S. ELIOT | FABER AND FABER LIMITED | 24 Russell Square | London

99 pp. 22½ × 15 cm. *5s.* Blue cloth lettered downward in gold on spine; end-papers. Red dust-wrapper printed in black.

'The three lectures which, with some revision and division, are here printed, were delivered in March 1939 at . . . Corpus Christi College, Cambridge, on the Boutwood Foundation'—*Preface*, p. 5.

2,000 copies were published on October 26, 1939. *On verso of title-page*: First published in October MCMXXXIX . . .

*b. First American edition ( [1940] ):*

The Idea of | a Christian Society | T. S. Eliot | HARCOURT, BRACE AND COMPANY | NEW YORK

vii, 104 pp. 22 × 15 cm. $1.50. Blue cloth lettered downward in gold on spine; end-papers. White dust-wrapper printed in blue.

3,000 copies were published on January 4, 1940. *On verso of title-page*: first American edition

A36          EAST COKER        1940

*a. First edition:*

THE NEW ENGLISH WEEKLY EASTER NUMBER, 1940 | (Supplement) | EAST COKER | I. | [*First page of text*. London, The New English Weekly]

pp. [325]–328. 32½ × 22½ cm. *1s.* Unbound.

The first separate appearance of the poem, issued after the edition of the complete number of *The New English Weekly* had been exhausted shortly before May 23, 1940. In its form as published in the original number, the Supplement measures approximately 31½ × 22 cm., and is held in place with two staples.

*b. Second edition:*

EAST COKER | A POEM BY | T. S. ELIOT | [*ornament*] | [London] Reprinted from the Easter Number | of the "New English Weekly," 1940.

8 pp. 21 × 16½ cm. 1s. Stapled.

500 copies were published by *The New English Weekly* shortly before June 13, 1940, in response to requests for copies of the Supplement.

*c. Third (first Faber) edition ([1940]):*

EAST COKER | by | T. S. ELIOT | FABER AND FABER | 24 Russell Square | London

1 blank leaf, 2 leaves, 7–15 pp. 22½ × 15 cm. 1s. Yellow paper wrappers printed in black, folded over stiff white paper; stapled.

9,030 copies were published on September 12, 1940. *On verso of title-page*: First published in September Mcmxl. . . . The poem was not published separately in the United States, but it was reprinted in *Four Quartets* [*by*] *T. S. Eliot* (New York, Harcourt, Brace [1943]), pp. [9]–17.

## A37            BURNT NORTON            [1941]

*First separate edition:*

BURNT NORTON | by | T. S. ELIOT | FABER AND FABER | 24 Russell Square | London

2 blank leaves, 2 leaves, 9–15 pp. 22½ × 15 cm. 1s. Green paper wrappers printed in black, folded over stiff white paper; stapled.

4,000 copies were published on February 20, 1941. *On verso of title-page*: First published in February Mcmxli. . . . Reprinted from *Collected Poems, 1909–1935* (1936). No separate edition was published in the United States, but the poem was included in *Four Quartets* ([1943]), pp. [1]–8.

## A38            POINTS OF VIEW            [1941]

*First edition:*

POINTS OF VIEW | by | T. S. ELIOT | FABER AND FABER LTD | 24 Russell Square | London

158 pp., 1 blank leaf. 19 × 13 cm. (Sesame Books) 3s. 6d. Blue cloth lettered in red on front cover and on spine; end-papers. Grey dust-wrapper printed in red.

4,000 copies were published on July 24, 1941. *On verso of title-page*: First published in June [*sic*] Mcmxli . . .

'This selection of T. S. Eliot's critical writings has been made and edited, with the author's approval, by John Hayward'—*Note*, p. 5. Nothing is printed here for the first time. This book has not been published in the United States.

**A39** THE DRY SALVAGES [1941]

*First edition:*

THE DRY SALVAGES | by | T. S. ELIOT | FABER AND FABER |
24 Russell Square | London

15 pp. $22\frac{1}{2} \times 15\frac{1}{2}$ cm. 1*s.* Blue paper wrappers printed in black,
folded over stiff cream or (later) blue, white, or grey, paper;
stapled.

11,223 copies were published on September 4, 1941. Late copies
of the first impression are printed on slightly thicker paper without
the watermark ADELPHI. *On verso of title-page*: First published in
September Mcmxli. . . . The poem was not separately published in
the United States, but it was reprinted in *Four Quartets* ([1943]),
pp. [19]–28.

**A40** THE MUSIC OF POETRY 1942

*First edition:*

THE MUSIC OF | POETRY | The third W. P. Ker Memorial
Lecture delivered | in the University of Glasgow | 24th February
1942 | by | T. S. ELIOT | A. M. (HARVARD); HON. LITT. D. (CAM-
BRIDGE, COLUMBIA, BRISTOL, LEEDS); | HON. LL.D. (EDINBURGH);
HON. FELLOW OF MAGDALENE COLLEGE, CAMBRIDGE | [*device*] | GLAS-
GOW | JACKSON, SON & COMPANY | PUBLISHERS TO THE
UNIVERSITY | 1942

28 pp. $21\frac{1}{2} \times 13\frac{1}{2}$ cm. (Glasgow University Publications, 57) 1*s.* 6*d.*
Tan paper wrappers printed in dark blue on front cover; stapled.

1,000 copies were published on August 30, 1942. This essay was
not separately published in the United States, but it was reprinted
in *Modern Writing* [*edited by*] *Willard Thorp . . . & Margaret
Farrand Thorp* (New York [&c.] American Book Company [1944]),
pp. 389–405, of which the first printing may be identified by the
code letters 'E.P.1' on the verso of the title-page.

**A41** THE CLASSICS AND 1942
THE MAN OF LETTERS

*First edition:*

THE CLASSICS | AND THE MAN OF LETTERS | by | T. S.
ELIOT | The Presidential Address delivered | to the Classical Associa-
tion | on 15 April 1942 | OXFORD UNIVERSITY PRESS | London
New York Toronto | 1942

27, [1] pp. 16 × 12½ cm. 8*d.* (25c.) Pale-blue paper wrappers printe
in black; blank leaves at front and back pasted down as end-papers
Published in August 1942.

## A42        LITTLE GIDDING      [1942

*First edition:*

LITTLE GIDDING | by | T. S. ELIOT | FABER AND FABER
24 Russell Square | London

    1 blank leaf, 2 leaves, 7–16 pp. 22½ × 15 cm. 1*s.* Stiff brown pape
wrappers; sewn or (later) stapled.

    16,775 copies were published on December 1, 1942. *On verso o
title-page*: First published in Mcmxlii. . . . The poem was no
separately published in the United States, but it was reprinted i
*Four Quartets* ([1943]), pp. [29]–39.

## A43    REUNION BY DESTRUCTION   [1943

*First edition:*

REUNION | BY DESTRUCTION | Reflections on a Scheme fo
Church Union | in South India: | Addressed to the Laity | by | T. S
ELIOT | [*device*] | The Council for | the Defence of | Church Principle
Pamphlet 7 [London, The Pax House, Dacre Street]

    cover-title, 21, [1] pp., 1 leaf. 18½ × 12 cm. (The Council for th
Defence of Church Principles, Pamphlet 7) 1*s.* Brown or (later) ta
paper wrappers; stapled.

    Published in November 1943. This pamphlet was not publishe
in the United States.

## A44       FOUR QUARTETS       [1943

*a. First edition:*[1]

FOUR | QUARTETS | T. S. ELIOT | NEW YORK | HARCOURT
BRACE AND COMPANY

    5 leaves, 3–39 pp. 22 × 15 cm. $2.00. Black cloth lettered downwar
in gold on spine; end-papers. White dust-wrapper (designed by
E. McKnight Kauffer) printed in black, cream, and grey.

    There were two impressions of this book before publication. The
first may be identified by the words 'first American edition' on the
verso of the title-page. In all the 4,165 copies of this first impression,

[1] i.e. the first collected edition of the four poems *Burnt Norton, East Coker
The Dry Salvages, Little Gidding*, for which see Nos. 36, 37, 39, 42 above.

the margins of many pages were incorrect because of faulty imposition of the formes as a result of unskilled war-time labour. The entire impression would have been destroyed except that it was necessary to meet the announced publication date (May 11,1943) in order to preserve copyright, and consequently 788 copies for review and other purposes were distributed before the formes could be correctly reimposed for a fresh impression. On May 5, 1943, the 3,377 copies of the first impression then remaining were destroyed and replaced by a second impression of 3,500 copies. These do not carry the edition note on the verso of the title-page. The book was officially published on May 11, 1943. Subsequent impressions may be identified by code designations within brackets on the verso of the title-page.

C o n t e n t s: Burnt Norton—East Coker—The Dry Salvages —Little Gidding.

*b. First English edition* ([*1944*]):

FOUR QUARTETS | by | T. S. ELIOT | FABER AND FABER | 24 Russell Square | London

44 pp. $22\frac{1}{2} \times 15$ cm. 6s. Tan cloth lettered downward in gold on spine; end-papers. Grey dust-wrapper printed in black and red.

6,000 copies were published on October 31, 1944. *On verso of title-page*: First published in this edition Mcmxliv . . .

# A45   WHAT IS A CLASSIC?   [1945]

*a. First edition, Virgil Society issue:*

WHAT IS A CLASSIC? | an address delivered before | the Virgil Society | on the | 16th of October | 1944 | by | T. S. ELIOT | FABER & FABER LIMITED | 24 Russell Square | London

32 pp. $23 \times 15\frac{1}{2}$ cm. Not for sale. Stiff green paper wrappers printed in black on front cover; stapled.

500 copies were published for distribution gratis to members of the Virgil Society. This issue contains 'The Virgil Society', a statement of the objects of the Society, signed by H. E. Butler, T. S. Eliot, and five others, pp. [3–4]. The text is the same as that of the ordinary issue. *On verso of title-page*: First published in Mcmxlv . . .

*b. Ordinary issue;*

1 blank leaf, 2 leaves, 7–32 pp. $22\frac{1}{2} \times 14\frac{1}{2}$ cm. 3s. 6d. Blue cloth lettered downward in gold on spine; end-papers. Cream dust-wrapper printed in black and red.

4,500 copies were published on February 2, 1945. *On verso of title-page*: First published in Mcmxlv . . .

## A46 DIE EINHEIT DER EUROPÄISCHEN KULTUR 1946

*First edition:*

T. S. ELIOT | DIE EINHEIT DER | EUROPÄISCHEN | KULTUR | BERLIN 1946 | CARL HABEL VERLAGSBUCHHANDLUNG

63, [1] pp. $19 \times 12\frac{1}{2}$ cm. Yellow paper wrappers printed in brown on front cover.

English and German texts printed on opposite pages.

'Die folgenden drei Vorträge wurden in der Sendereihe 'Lebendiges Abendland' des Deutschen Dienstes des Londoner Rundfunks am 10., 17. und 24. März 1946 nach der hier neben dem englischen Originaltext wiedergegebenen deutschen Fassung gesprochen, der Anfang und der Schluss vom Verfasser selber. Die Übersetzung stammt von Leonie Hiller'—*Note*, p. [3].

This book was not published in England or the United States, but the English text was printed as an appendix in both English and American editions of *Notes towards the Definition of Culture*.

'T. S. Eliot, von Hans Hennecke': pp. 61–[64].

## A47 A PRACTICAL POSSUM 1947

*First edition:*

A PRACTICAL | POSSUM | [*row of ornaments in green*] | by T. S. ELIOT | [*row of ornaments in green*] | HARVARD PRINTING OFFICE AND | DEPARTMENT OF GRAPHIC ARTS | CAMBRIDGE: MCMXLVII

[7] pp. $23\frac{1}{2} \times 15$ cm. Not for sale. Grey-green paper wrappers printed in black on front cover; sewn.

*Colophon* (*p.* [7]): . . . The edition is limited to eighty copies, of which this copy is number . . .

Issued June 19, 1947. Printed under the direction of Philip Hofer by a class of student printers in the Department of Graphic Arts at Harvard. The size of the edition was subsequently reduced from eighty copies to the sixty authorized, by the calling-in of twenty copies, which were handed over to the author. *On verso of title-page*: First edition. At the request of the author, no copies are for sale.

A48                   ON POETRY                   1947

*First edition:*

ON | Poetry | AN ADDRESS BY T. S. ELIOT | ON THE | OCCA-
SION OF THE TWENTY-FIFTH ANNIVERSARY | OF | CON-
CORD ACADEMY | . | CONCORD, MASSACHUSETTS | June
3, 1947

　　15, [1] pp. 18 × 13 cm. Not for sale. Olive-green paper wrappers
printed in grey and green; stapled.
　　750 copies were printed by Whittet & Shepperson, Richmond,
Virginia, and distributed gratis to alumnae and friends of Concord
Academy in October and November 1947. Each copy is numbered in
ink on the inside front cover.

A49                    MILTON                     1947

*First edition:*

MILTON | By | T. S. ELIOT | ANNUAL LECTURE ON A
MASTER MIND | HENRIETTE HERTZ TRUST | of the |
BRITISH ACADEMY | 1947 | Price 2s. 6d. net | FROM THE PRO-
CEEDINGS OF THE | BRITISH ACADEMY. VOLUME XXXIII
| LONDON : GEOFFREY CUMBERLEGE . | AMEN HOUSE,
E.C.4

　　cover-title, 19, [1] pp. 26 × 16½ cm. *2s. 6d.* Grey paper wrappers
printed in black on pages [1, 2, and 4] of cover; sewn.
　　'Read 26 March 1947'
　　500 copies were published on October 23, 1947. It was reprinted
in Volume 33 of the *Proceedings of the British Academy* (London, G.
Cumberlege, Oxford University Press [1951]), pp. [61]–79,
published on November 29, 1951. The essay has not been separately
published in the United States.

A50                   A SERMON                    1948

*First edition:*

A SERMON | preached in | Magdalene College Chapel | by | T. S.
ELIOT, o. m. | HONORARY FELLOW | [*device*] | 7 MARCH 1948
[*all the above within border of thick and thin rule.* Cambridge, Printed
at the University Press]

　　7, [1] pp. 18½ × 12½ cm. Not for sale. Unbound; stapled.
　　500 copies were distributed gratis to members of the College in
June 1948.

A51 NOTES TOWARDS THE [1948]
DEFINITION OF CULTURE

*a. First edition:*

Notes towards | the Definition of Culture | by | T. S. ELIOT | [*quotation in three lines*] | FABER AND FABER LIMITED | 24 Russell Square | London

1 blank leaf, 3 leaves, 9–124 pp., 2 blank leaves. $22\frac{1}{2} \times 15$ cm. 10*s.* 6*d.* Blue cloth lettered in gold on spine; front end-paper (final blank leaf pasted down as back end-paper). Cream dust-wrapper printed in red and black.

6,000 copies were published in November 1948. (A few proof copies in yellow paper wrappers were made up for the publishers before publication.) Eighteen copies were bound, in cloth, with the error 'a' for 'the' in the title on the spine, but none of these was put on sale by the publishers. *On verso of title-page*: First published in mcmxlviii . . .

CONTENTS: Introduction—The Three Senses of 'Culture'—The Class and the Elite—Unity and Diversity: The Region—Unity and Diversity: Sect and Cult—A Note on Culture and Politics—Notes on Education and Culture: and Conclusion—Appendix–The Unity of European Culture

*b. First American edition ([1949]):*

[*Rule*] | Notes towards the | DEFINITION | OF CULTURE | [*rule*] | T. S. ELIOT | [*quotation in three lines*] | [*rule*] | HARCOURT, BRACE AND COMPANY | NEW YORK

128 pp. $22 \times 15$ cm. $2.50. Black cloth lettered downward in gold on spine; end-papers. White dust-wrapper printed in grey and turquoise.

7,500 copies were published on March 3, 1949. *On verso of title-page*: first American edition

A52 FROM POE TO VALERY [1948]

*a. First edition:*

[*In green:*] FROM POE | TO VALERY | [*in black:*] T. S. ELIOT | HARCOURT, BRACE AND COMPANY | NEW YORK [*all the above within single rule border in black*]

32 pp. $19\frac{1}{2} \times 12\frac{1}{2}$ cm. Not for sale. Dark-blue paper boards stamped in white and green (with design by E. McKnight Kauffer); grey end-papers. Issued in green mailing envelope.

*Colophon* (*p.* [1]): MCMXLIX  This first edition of "From Poe to Valéry" is limited to fifteen hundred copies privately printed for the friends of the author and his publishers as a New Year's Greeting.

Copyrighted December 20, 1948. Originally delivered as a lecture at the Library of Congress, November 19, 1948.

*b. Second edition* (*1949*):

[*Coat of Arms*] | FROM POE TO VALÉRY | A Lecture Delivered | at the | LIBRARY OF CONGRESS | On Friday, November 19, 1948 | by | T. S. ELIOT | Washington | 1949

cover-title, 16 pp. 25 × 17 cm.. Not for sale. Stiff white paper wrappers printed in black; stapled.

Distributed gratis in December 1949, by the Library of Congress Information and Publication Office. *On verso of cover-title*: Reprinted from *The Hudson Review*, Volume II, Number 3, Autumn, 1949.

## A53  THE UNDERGRADUATE [1949] POEMS

*First edition:*

The | Undergraduate | Poems | of T. S. ELIOT | [*device*] | published while he was at college in | The Harvard Advocate | 40 Bow Street | Cambridge 38, Massachusetts

cover-title, 7, [1] pp. .23 × 13½ cm. 35c. Grey paper wrappers printed in black; stapled.

An edition of about 1,000 copies was published, without authorization, early in 1949. Of these copies about 750 were withdrawn from circulation in December 1949. Reprinted from *The Harvard Advocate*, November, 1948, with changes in order and with the addition of one poem, but without the correction of the several serious misprints.

CONTENTS: Song ['When we came [home] across the hill']—Song ['If space and time, as sages say']—Before Morning—Circe's Palace —Song ['The moonflower opens to the moth']—On a Portrait— Nocturne—Spleen—Humo[u]resque—[Class] Ode.

## A54  THE AIMS OF 1949 POETIC DRAMA

*First edition:*

THE AIMS OF | POETIC DRAMA | THE PRESIDENTIAL ADDRESS TO | THE POETS' THEATRE GUILD | T. S. ELIOT | 1949 | SIXPENCE [London, The Poets' Theatre Guild]

7, [1] pp. $21\frac{1}{2} \times 14$ cm. *6d.* Unbound; stapled.

5,000 copies were printed for the Guild by the Galleon Press, Croydon, for distribution gratis to members in August 1949, and for sale.

A55     THE COCKTAIL PARTY     [1950]

*a. First edition:*

THE | COCKTAIL PARTY | a comedy by | T. S. ELIOT | FABER AND FABER LTD | 24 Russell Square | London

167, [1] pp., 2 leaves (incl. music), 2 blank leaves. $22\frac{1}{2} \times 14\frac{1}{2}$ cm. 10*s.* 6*d.* Green cloth stamped in gold on spine; end-papers. Grey dust-wrapper printed in black and red.

19,950 copies were published on March 9, 1950. A number of copies (a few hundred at most) have a misprint 'here' for 'her' in line 1, page 29, which was overlooked in the page-proof, but corrected in the press after these copies had been bound. Copies with and without the error were bound up and issued simultaneously. (The first copy delivered to the publishers, as also the wrappered proof copies, did not contain the error.) The whole edition had unexpectedly to be rushed through the press, during the author's absence in South Africa, in order to coincide with the production of the play in New York and the publication of the American edition. (A few proof copies in grey paper wrappers were made up for the publishers before publication.) *On verso of title-page*: First published in mcml . . .

*b. First American edition:*

The Cocktail Party | a comedy by | T. S. ELIOT | Harcourt, Brace and Company, New York

190, [2] pp., incl. music. $22 \times 15$ cm. $3.00. Black cloth lettered downward in gold on spine; end-papers. White dust-wrapper printed in yellow and black.

10,000 copies were published on March 10, 1950. These have pages 35–36 cancelled and replaced with a new leaf correcting an error in the attribution of the last two speeches on page 35. The publishers state that 'about ten copies (at most)' escaped cancellation. (A few sets of the page proofs, containing the error, in pale blue paper wrappers, were distributed as advance copies. These have certain other variations from the published text.) Through oversight, the words 'first American edition' were omitted from the verso of the title-page on the first printing. Second and subsequent impressions may be identified by code symbols.

A56 POEMS WRITTEN IN 1950
EARLY YOUTH

*First edition:*

Poems | written in early | youth | by | T. S. Eliot | PRIVATELY
PRINTED | STOCKHOLM | 1950

1 blank leaf, 3 leaves, 9–41, [1] pp., 1 blank leaf, 1 leaf, 1 blank leaf.
20 × 12½ cm. Not for sale. White paper boards with green paper
labels printed in black on front cover and on spine; end-papers.

*Colophon* (*p.* [45]): This collection of poems, written in early youth
by T. S. Eliot, was compiled by John Hayward and privately printed,
with the author's permission, in December 1950, at the charge of
Georg Svensson and his colleagues in the publishing house of
Bonniers, Stockholm, in an edition limited to twelve copies, numbered 1–12. This copy is No: . . .

'⟨At Graduation 1905⟩' and 'The Death of Saint Narcissus' were
printed here for the first time; the first from the only surviving
typescript, in the possession of John Hayward, the second from a
unique corrected galley-proof for *Poetry* (Chicago), in the Harriet
Monroe Collection, University of Chicago Library.

CONTENTS: Introduction [signed: J. H.]—A fable for feasters—
⟨A lyric:⟩ 'If Time and Space, as Sages say'—Song: 'If space and
time, as sages say'— ⟨At graduation 1905⟩—Song: 'When we came
home across the hill'—Before Morning—Circe's Palace—On a
Portrait—Song: 'The moonflower opens to the moth'—Nocturne—
Humouresque (after J. Laforgue)—Spleen—[Class] Ode—The
Death of Saint Narcissus—Notes [by J. H.].

A57 POETRY AND DRAMA 1951

*a. First edition:*

T. S. ELIOT | POETRY AND DRAMA | HARVARD UNIVERSITY
PRESS · CAMBRIDGE, MASSACHUSETTS | nineteen fifty-one

3 leaves, [3]–44 pp. 19½ × 14 cm. $1.50. Dark-blue cloth lettered
downward in gold on spine; end-papers. White dust-wrapper
printed in blue, black, and brown, with yellow oval label printed in
dark brown pasted on front, and reproduction on back of a drawing
of the author by his sister-in-law Theresa Garrett Eliot (Mrs.
Henry Ware Eliot, Jr.).

5,000 copies were published on March 15, 1951.

'The Theodore Spencer Memorial Lecture, November 21, 1950.'
Based, in part, upon an earlier lecture which was delivered to
European audiences in 1949 and printed in November of that year
in the periodical *Adam* with title, 'The Aims of Poetic Drama'.

# A. *Books and Pamphlets*

*b. First English edition* ([*1951*]):

POETRY | AND | DRAMA | by | T. S. ELIOT | The Theodore
Spencer Memorial Lecture | HARVARD UNIVERSITY | November 21,
1950 | FABER & FABER LTD | 24 Russell Square | London

1 blank leaf, 2 leaves, 7–35 pp., 2 blank leaves. $22\frac{1}{2} \times 14\frac{1}{2}$ cm. 7*s*. 6*d*.
Red cloth lettered downward in gold on spine; end-papers. Blue
dust-wrapper printed in red.

10,000 copies were published on September 28, 1951. *On verso of
title-page*: First published in mcmli . . .

# B

BOOKS AND
PAMPHLETS EDITED, OR
WITH CONTRIBUTIONS, BY
T. S. ELIOT

**B1**             'THE [CLASS] ODE'           [1910]

HARVARD | CLASS DAY | 1910 | [*Arms of Harvard College*. Cambridge, Mass.]

cover-title, 17 leaves. illus. 17 × 12 cm. Stiff cream paper wrappers stamped in blind and lettered in gold, punched and tied with red cord.

Published for distribution gratis to members of the Class of 1910 and their guests on June 24, 1910.

Contains 'The [Class] Ode', by Thomas Stearns Eliot: fourth leaf.

**B2**        CATHOLIC ANTHOLOGY          1915

CATHOLIC | ANTHOLOGY | 1914–1915 | [*device*] | LONDON | ELKIN MATHEWS, CORK STREET | 1915

vii, 99, [1] pp. 19½ × 13 cm. *3s. 6d.* Grey paper boards printed in black; end-papers.

Edited by Ezra Pound. Published in November 1915.

Contains 'The Love Song of J. Alfred Prufrock', 'Portrait of a Lady', 'The Boston Evening Transcript', 'Hysteria', and 'Miss Helen Slingsby': pp. 2–17. This is the first appearance in book-form of any of T. S. Eliot's verse. The final poem was reprinted as 'Aunt Helen'.

**B3**                 OTHERS                  1916

OTHERS | AN ANTHOLOGY OF THE NEW VERSE | EDITED BY | ALFRED KREYMBORG | [*device*] | [*rule*] | NEW YORK [*ornament*] ALFRED A KNOPF [*ornament*] MCMXVI

4 leaves, 152 pp. 21 × 13 cm. $1.50. Brown paper boards printed in red; end-papers. Dust-wrapper.

*On verso of title-page:* Published March [25], 1916.

Contains 'Portrait of a Lady': pp. 33–38. This is the first appearance in book-form in America of any of T. S. Eliot's verse.

**B4**          'ANDREW MARVELL'            1922

ANDREW MARVELL | 1621–1678 | Tercentenary Tributes | BY | [*names of eight contributors in five lines*] | EDITED, WITH AN OFFICIAL RECORD OF THE TERCENTENARY | CELEBRA- TIONS AT KINGSTON-UPON-HULL AND IN | LONDON, BY | WM. H. BAGGULEY, F.L.A. | CITY LIBRARIAN, HULL | Por- traits and other Illustrations | HUMPHREY MILFORD | OXFORD UNIVERSITY PRESS | LONDON EDINBURGH GLASGOW

COPENHAGEN | NEW YORK TORONTO MELBOURNE CAPE
TOWN | BOMBAY CALCUTTA MADRAS SHANGHAI | 1922

131, [1] pp. front.(port.), illus. (incl. facsim.), plates, ports.
$19\frac{1}{2} \times 13\frac{1}{2}$ cm. 6s. Blue cloth stamped in blind and gold on front
cover and in gold on spine; end-papers.
1,000 copies were published on May 22, 1922.
Contains 'Andrew Marvell, by T. S. Eliot, M.A.': pp. [63]–78.

B5            'DORIS'S           [1924]
DREAM SONGS'

THE CHAPBOOK | A MISCELLANY | (No. 39) | 1924 | [*device*] |
THE POETRY BOOKSHOP | 35 DEVONSHIRE STREET |
THEOBALDS ROAD | LONDON, W.C.1

71, [1] pp. illus. $22\frac{1}{2} \times 18$ cm. 3s. 6d. Cream paper boards printed in
pink, blue, and green; end-papers.
Published in November 1924.
Contains 'Doris's Dream Songs', three poems, by T. S. Eliot, with
a decoration by E. McKnight Kauffer: pp. 36–37. The poems begin
respectively 'Eyes that last I saw in tears', 'The wind sprang up at
four o'clock', and 'This is the dead land'. Reprinted as 'Three
Dream Songs', in *American Poetry 1925, A Miscellany* (New York,
Harcourt, Brace [1925]), pp. 67–69, which was published in August
1925. The third poem was used as Part III of 'The Hollow Men'.

B6            'A BRIEF           [1924]
INTRODUCTION TO THE
METHOD OF PAUL VALÉRY'

[*In red:*] LE SERPENT | [*in black:*] PAR | PAUL VALERY | WITH
A TRANSLATION INTO | ENGLISH BY MARK WARDLE |
AND AN INTRODUCTION BY | T. S. ELIOT | PUBLISHED FOR
THE CRITERION | BY R. COBDEN-SANDERSON | 17 THAVIES
INN | LONDON

51 pp. $23 \times 15$ cm. 10s. 6d. Black cloth stamped in red on front cover
and downward on spine; end-papers. Cream dust-wrapper printed in
red and black.
*Colophon* (*p.* [2]): Five hundred and twenty-five copies of this
edition have been printed, of which five hundred are for sale. This is
No. . . .
Published in December 1924.
'A Brief Introduction to the Method of Paul Valéry': pp. 7–15.

## B. *Contributions to Books*

**B7**               'THE HOLLOW               [1925]
                     MEN [PART I]'

THE BEST POEMS | OF 1925 | EDITED BY | L. A. G. STRONG |
Author of 'Dublin Days' | Editor of 'The Best Poems of 1923' and |
'The Best Poems of 1924' | [*device*] | BOSTON | SMALL, MAY-
NARD & COMPANY | PUBLISHERS

> xxix pp., 1 leaf, 248 pp. 17 × 12 cm. Blue cloth stamped in gold on
> front cover and on spine; end-papers.
>> Published on November 18, 1925.
>> Contains 'The Hollow Men [Part 1]' by T. S. Eliot: p. 69.

**B8**               SAVONAROLA               [1926]

SAVONAROLA | A DRAMATIC POEM | By CHARLOTTE ELIOT
| With an Introduction by | T. S. ELIOT | LONDON | R. COBDEN-
SANDERSON | 17 THAVIES INN, E.C.

> xv, 99 pp. 19½ × 14 cm. 5s. ( $1.75). Black cloth with white paper
> label printed in black on spine; end-papers. Grey dust-wrapper
> printed in black.
>> 300 copies were published early in March 1926. Copies were
>> imported in the autumn of 1926 for sale in Boston, Cambridge, and
>> New York.
>> 'Introduction': pp. vii–xii.

**B9**               ['SENECA IN               1927
            ELIZABETHAN TRANSLATION']

[*In red:*] SENECA | [*in black:*] HIS TENNE TRAGEDIES | TRANS-
LATED INTO ENGLISH | EDITED BY | THOMAS NEWTON |
ANNO 1581 | With an Introduction by | T. S. ELIOT | [*in red:*]
FIRST [-SECOND] VOLUME | [*in black: device*] | LONDON:
CONSTABLE AND CO. LTD. | NEW YORK: ALFRED A. KNOPF
| 1927

> *Volume 1*: 1 blank leaf, liv, 231 pp.; *Volume 2*: 2 leaves, 257 pp.,
> 1 blank leaf. 21½ × 16½ cm. (The Tudor Translations, Second Series;
> ed. by Charles Whibley, XI) 42s. ( $8.00). Maroon paper boards
> with red buckram backs stamped in gold; top edges gilt or plain;
> maroon end-papers.

*Colophon* (*v.* 1, *p.* [ii]): This edition is limited to 1,025 copies Published in September 1927. Copies for sale in England had top edges gilt.

'Introduction': v. 1, pp. v–liv. Reprinted as 'Seneca in Elizabethan translation'.

B10     ['WILKIE COLLINS     [1928]
### AND DICKENS']

THE MOONSTONE | BY | WILKIE COLLINS | WITH | AN INTRODUCTION BY | T. S. ELIOT | [*device*] | OXFORD UNIVERSITY PRESS | HUMPHREY MILFORD

xx, 522 pp., 1 leaf. 15½ × 10 cm. (The World's Classics, 316) 2*s*. Green cloth stamped in blind or blue cloth stamped in blind and gold on front cover, both stamped in blind on back cover and in blind and gold on spine; end-papers. White dust-wrapper printed in blue with portrait of Collins. (Some copies have sixteen pages of inserted advertisements at the end. A later binding in blue cloth has dust-wrapper with world map, and advertisements dated July 1931.)

5,000 copies were published on March 1, 1928. *On verso of title-page*: . . . first published in 1928.

'Introduction': pp. [v]–xii. Reprinted as 'Wilkie Collins and Dickens'.

B11     'A DIALOGUE ON     1928
### POETIC DRAMA'

*a. Signed issue:*

Of | DRAMATICK POESIE | AN ESSAY | 1668 | by JOHN DRYDEN | Preceded by a | DIALOGUE | on POETIC DRAMA | by T. S. ELIOT | LONDON | Frederick Etchells & Hugh Macdonald | 1928 [*all the above within border of type ornaments*]

xxvi, [1], 83, [1] pp. 30½ × 20 cm. (The Haslewood Books) 63*s*. White buckram stamped in gold on front cover, with tan vellum back lettered downward in gold on spine; end-papers.

*Colophon* (*p.* [iv]): Of this edition printed in England by Richard Clay & Sons, Ltd., 580 numbered copies are for sale, of which numbers 1 to 55 have been printed on Millbourn hand-made paper. This is number . . . [*signed*] T. S. Eliot.

Published in May 1928.

'A Dialogue on Poetic Drama': pp. xi–[xxvii]. Reprinted as A Dialogue on Dramatic Poetry'.

*b. Ordinary issue:*

31*s.* 6*d.* Marbled paper boards with blue buckram back lettered downward in gold on spine; end-papers. Grey dust-wrapper printed in black.

Colophon as above, but unsigned.

## B12      THIS AMERICAN WORLD      [1928]

THIS | AMERICAN WORLD | by | Edgar Ansel Mowrer | with a preface by | T. S. Eliot | LONDON | Faber & Gwyer

xv, 17–254 pp., 1 blank leaf. 21 × 14½ cm. 7*s.* 6*d.* Green cloth lettered in gold on spine; end-papers. Cream dust-wrapper printed in green.

1,000 copies were published on September 17, 1928. *On verso of title-page*: First published in MCMXXVIII . . .

'Preface': pp. ix–xv.

## B13      FISHERMEN      [1928]
## OF THE BANKS

FISHERMEN | of the | BANKS | by | JAMES B. CONNOLLY | illustrated by | HENRY O'CONNOR | LONDON | Faber & Gwyer

xi, 13–274, [1] pp., incl. front., illus., plates. 22½ × 15½ cm. 12*s.* 6*d.* Blue cloth stamped in gold on front cover and on spine; end-papers. Grey dust-wrapper printed in blue.

1,000 copies were published on October 4, 1928. *On verso of title-page*: First published in MCMXXVIII . . .

Contains 'Publishers' Preface' by T. S. Eliot, anonymously: pp. vii–viii.

## B14      EZRA POUND      [1928]
## SELECTED POEMS

*a. First edition, ordinary issue:*

EZRA POUND | [*ornament*] | SELECTED POEMS | EDITED WITH AN INTRODUCTION | BY | T. S. ELIOT | * | THIS SELECTION INCLUDES | PERSONÆ OF EZRA POUND | RIPOSTES | LUSTRA | CATHAY | H. S. MAUBERLEY | AND SOME EARLY POEMS | REJECTED BY THE AUTHOR | AND OMITTED FROM | HIS COLLECTED EDITION | * | LONDON | FABER & GWYER

1 blank leaf, 2 leaves, vii–xxxii, 184 pp. 19½ × 14 cm. 7*s. 6d.* Green cloth stamped in gold on spine; end-papers. Tan dust-wrapper printed in black. (A later binding gives the name of the publishers, on the spine, as Faber & Faber.)

1,000 copies were published on November 23, 1928. *On verso of title-page*: First published in MCMXXVIII. . . . This book was not published in the United States, Boni & Liveright having published another collection in New York in 1926.

*b. Signed issue:*

xxxii, 184 pp. 20½ × 14½ cm. 25*s.* Grey paper boards with white vellum back stamped in gold; end-papers. Glacine dust-wrapper.

*Colophon* (*p.* [ii]): This edition printed on English hand-made paper is limited to one hundred numbered copies. This is number . . . [*signed*] E. Pound

Published on December 10, 1928.

*c. New edition* ([*1948*]):

EZRA POUND | [*ornament*] | SELECTED POEMS | EDITED WITH AN | INTRODUCTION | BY | T. S. ELIOT | FABER AND FABER | 24 Russell Square | London

1 blank leaf, 2 leaves, 7–199 pp. 21 × 14 cm. 12*s. 6d.* Green cloth stamped in gold on spine; end-papers. Grey dust-wrapper printed in green and red.

*On verso of title-page*: First published in mcmxxviii Reissued in this new edition mcmxlviii. . . . This edition was published in the United States by New Directions.

Contains 'Introduction: 1928', signed: T. S. Eliot, pp. 7–21, and 'Postscript: 1948', signed: T. S. E., p. 21.

## B15    'EXPERIMENT IN    1929 CRITICISM'

TRADITION AND | EXPERIMENT | IN PRESENT-DAY LITERATURE | ADDRESSES DELIVERED | AT THE CITY LITERARY | INSTITUTE | 1929 | OXFORD UNIVERSITY PRESS | LONDON: HUMPHREY MILFORD

4 leaves, 215, [1] pp. 20 × 13½ cm. 7*s. 6d.* Green cloth lettered in gold on front cover and on spine; end-papers. Yellow dust-wrapper printed in black.

2,000 copies were published on November 25, 1929. Of these, 561 sets of sheets were imported and published by the Oxford University Press, New York.

Contains 'Experiment in Criticism, by T. S. Eliot': pp. [198]–215.

## B. *Contributions to Books*

**B16**  'RELIGION  [1930]
WITHOUT HUMANISM'

HUMANISM | AND | AMERICA | ESSAYS | ON THE OUTLOOK | OF MODERN CIVILISATION | Edited by | NORMAN FOERSTER | [*device*] | FARRAR AND RINEHART | INCORPORATED | PUBLISHERS   NEW YORK

> xvii pp., 3 leaves, 3–294 pp. 22½ × 15½ cm. $3.50. Blue cloth stamped in gold on spine; end-papers.
> 2,250 copies were published on February 21, 1930. Publishers' monogram on verso of title-page.
> Contains 'Religion without Humanism [by] T. S. Eliot': pp. 105–12.

**B17**  THE WHEEL OF FIRE  1930

The Wheel of Fire | ESSAYS IN INTERPRETATION | OF SHAKE-SPEARE'S SOMBRE | TRAGEDIES | By G. WILSON KNIGHT | [*two quotations in nine lines between two ornaments*] | Oxford University Press | LONDON: HUMPHREY MILFORD | 1930

> xix, 296 pp. 22½ × 15½ cm. 12*s.* 6*d.* Brown cloth lettered in gold on front cover and on spine; end-papers. Grey-blue dust-wrapper printed in black.
> 1,500 copies were published on July 25, 1930.
> Contains 'Introduction', by T. S. Eliot: pp. [xi]–xix.

**B18**  ['BAUDELAIRE']  1930

*a. Ordinary issue:*

Charles Baudelaire | INTIMATE JOURNALS | TRANSLATED BY CH. ISHERWOOD | INTRODUCTION BY | T. S. Eliot | THE BLACKAMORE PRESS LONDON | RANDOM HOUSE NEW YORK | 1930 [*all the above within triple-ruled border*]

> 125, [3] pp. front.(port.), plates, ports. 21 × 15½ cm. 21*s.* Blue cloth stamped in gold on front cover with facsimile of Baudelaire's signature and upward on spine; end-papers. Cellophane dust-wrapper. Cardboard case.
> *Colophon* (*p.* [5]): This first English edition of the Intimate Journals consists of 400 copies, including 50 copies specially bound, signed by T. S. Eliot, for sale in England by the Blackamore Press, and 250 copies for sale in the United States by Random House Inc.; the

text has been printed by the Westminster Press in London, and the illustrations, reproducing Ch. Baudelaire's drawings, by D. Jacomet in Paris; all under the care of J. E. Pouterman   This is number . . .

Published in September 1930.

'Introduction': pp. 7–26. Reprinted as 'Baudelaire'.

*b. Signed issue:*

84*s*. Tan cloth stamped in gold with facsimile of Baudelaire's signature on front cover and with title upward on spine; end-papers. Cellophane dust-wrapper. Cardboard case.

Colophon as above, but signed: T. S. Eliot

Published in October 1930.

## B19      'THE PLACE OF PATER'      1930

THE | EIGHTEEN-EIGHTIES | Essays | by Fellows of | the Royal Society of | Literature | [*thick-thin rule*] | Edited by | WALTER DE LA MARE | [*thin-thick rule*] | Cambridge | AT THE UNIVERSITY PRESS | 1930

xxviii, 271 pp. 23 × 15 cm. 12*s*. 6*d*. Green cloth stamped in gold on spine; end-papers. Cream dust-wrapper printed in green and black.

2,500 copies were published in December 1930. The English sheets were imported and published in New York by Macmillan.

Contains 'The Place of Pater, by T. S. Eliot': pp. [93]–106. (As a contributor, T. S. Eliot received a few off-prints of this essay in plain grey paper wrappers. He renounced the title of F.R.S.L. after the payment of one year's dues.) Reprinted as 'Arnold and Pater'.

## B20      LONDON: A POEM AND      1930
## THE VANITY OF HUMAN WISHES

*a. Signed issue:*

LONDON : A POEM | AND | THE VANITY OF HUMAN | WISHES | BY | SAMUEL JOHNSON, LL. D. | WITH | AN INTRO-DUCTORY ESSAY | BY | T. S. ELIOT | [*ornament*] | LONDON | Frederick Etchells & Hugh Macdonald | 192 CHURCH STREET, W. 8 | M.CM.XXX

2 blank leaves, 44 pp., 1 leaf, 1 blank leaf. 35 × 22 cm. (The Haslewood Books) 21*s*. Tan paper boards with blue paper label on front cover printed in black; end-papers.

*Colophon* (*p*. [5]): Of this edition, printed in England by the Chiswick Press, 450 numbered copies have been issued of which 150, numbered 1 to 150 and signed by Mr. Eliot, have been printed on Kentish Rag paper. This is number . . . [*signed*] T. S. Eliot

Published in the autumn of 1930. According to advertisements, only fifty of the signed copies were for sale in England.

'Introductory Essay': pp. [9]–17. Reprinted as 'Johnson's *London* and *The Vanity of Human Wishes*', in *English Critical Essays: Twentieth Century; selected . . . by Phyllis M. Jones* (London, New York, Toronto, H. Milford, Oxford University Press [1933]), pp. 301–10. (World's Classics, 405).

*b. Ordinary issue:*

10s. 6d. Grey paper boards with buff paper label on front cover printed in black; end-papers.

Colophon as above, but unsigned.

# B21 ['THE PENSÉES OF PASCAL'] [1931]

*a. First issue*

[*Ornament*] PASCAL'S | PENSÉES [*ornament*] | TRANSLATED by | W. F. TROTTER | [*ornament*] | LONDON & TORONTO | PUBLISHED BY J·M·DENT | & SONS LTD & IN NEW YORK | BY E·P·DUTTON & CO [*all the above within ornamental border*]

xix pp., 1 leaf, 297, [1] pp. $17\frac{1}{2} \times 11$ cm. (Everyman's Library, 874) 2s. (90c.). Slate cloth stamped in blind on front cover and in gold on spine; decorated end-papers.. Yellow dust-wrapper printed in black.

Published on September 19, 1931, as part of a total first printing of 9,000 copies. (Also issued at 3s. ($1.00) in a 'library binding' of grey cloth stamped in blind on front cover and in blind and gold on spine; plain end-papers. Yellow dust-wrapper printed in green.) *On verso of title-page*: First published in this edition . 1931

Contains 'Introduction', by T. S. Eliot: pp. vii–xix. Reprinted as 'The *Pensées* of Pascal'.

*b. Second issue ([1936]):*

PENSEES | [*device*] | BLAISE PASCAL | LONDON: J. M. DENT & SONS LTD. | NEW YORK: E. P. DUTTON & CO. INC.

A second issue, with revised title, as above, was published in 1936, in similar binding and at the same price, with 15, [1] pp. of inserted advertisements at the end. The 'library binding' for the second issue was similar to that for the first issue, except that the spine was stamped in gold only and less elaborately; the price was unchanged.

B22 TRANSIT OF VENUS 1931

[*In red:*] TRANSIT OF VENUS | [*in black:*] POEMS | by | [*in red:*] Harry Crosby | [*in black:*] With a Preface by T. S. Eliot | The Black Sun Press | Rue Cardinale | Paris | [*in red:*] MCMXXXI

1 blank leaf, 2 leaves, ix, [3] pp., 1 leaf, 62 pp., 3 leaves, 1 blank leaf. 23 × 18 cm. ([Collected Poems of Harry Crosby, Vol. II].) For sale only with vols. I, III, IV, at $15.00. Stiff white paper wrappers printed in red and black on front cover and in red on spine, folded over blank leaves; sewn. Folded cellophane dust-wrapper. Issued with vols. I, II, IV as a set, in red cloth case.

*Colophon* (*recto of second leaf following p.* 62): This edition of Transit of Venus by Harry Crosby, with a preface by T. S. Eliot, being Volume II of the Collected Poems of Harry Crosby, is printed in hand-set dorique type at the Black Sun Press, Paris, 1931, under the direction of and for Caresse Crosby and is strictly limited to twenty lettered copies on Japanese Vellum and fifty numbered copies on Holland Paper together with the sheets for five hundred copies on uncut Navarre.

Mr. Harry F. Marks, the American agent for this edition, states that to the best of his knowledge, the sets on Japanese vellum were never issued, and that it is doubtful that the full fifty copies on Holland (announced to sell at $40 the set bound) were printed. At least several of the Navarre copies were numbered, in some instances with numbers between one and fifty theoretically reserved for the Holland paper sets.

'Preface': pp. i–ix. 'Books by Harry Crosby': third leaf following p. 62.

B23 'DONNE IN OUR TIME' 1931

A GARLAND | FOR | John Donne | 1631–1931 | [*double rule*] | EDITED BY | THEODORE SPENCER | [*double rule*] | CAM-BRIDGE | Harvard University Press | 1931 [*all the above within ornamental border*]

5 leaves, [3]–202 pp., 1 blank leaf. front.(port.) 21 × 14½ cm. $2.50. Red cloth stamped in blind on covers and in gold on spine; end-papers. Cream dust-wrapper printed in black, with reproduction of title-page on front cover dated 1931. (A later dust-wrapper is dated 1932).

Published on December 1, 1931. Issued in England in February 1932 by the Oxford University Press.

Contains 'Donne in Our Time [by] Thomas Stearns Eliot': pp. [1]–19.

# B24    BUBU OF MONTPARNASSE    1932

Bubu | of Montparnasse | by | Charles-Louis Philippe | Translated by
Laurence Vail | Preface by | T. S. Eliot | PARIS | Crosby Continental
Editions | 2, Rue Cardinale | 1932

> 1 blank leaf, 2 leaves, vii–xiv pp., 1 leaf, 17–218, [2] pp. 16½ × 12½ cm.
> (Modern Masterpieces in English, No. 4) 12 fr. White paper
> wrappers printed in blue.
>     *Colophon* (*p.* [220]): Published by the Black Sun Press . . . March
> 1932
>     'Preface': pp. vii–xiv. This preface was first published in the United
> States in *Bubu of Montparnasse by Charles-Louis Philippe in a New
> Redaction; Preface by T. S. Eliot* (New York, Avalon Press, 1945),
> pp. [7]–14.

# B25    'FRAGMENT OF AN AGON'    1932

[*In black:*] EZRA POUND | [*in red:*] PROFILE | [*in black:*]
AN ANTHOLOGY COLLECTED IN MCMXXXI | MILAN
MCMXXXII

> 1 blank leaf, 3 leaves, 9–142 pp., 3 leaves. 21 × 16 cm. Grey paper
> wrappers folded over stiff white paper, printed in black.
>     *Colophon* (*recto of third leaf following p. 142*): Edition privately
> printed for John Scheiwiller limited to 250 numbered copies.
> Copy N. . . .
>     Contains 'Fragment of an Agon (From *Wanna Go Home, Baby?*)',
> by T. S. Eliot: pp. 91–99.

# B26    'FROM T. S. ELIOT'    [1933]

THE CANTOS | of | EZRA POUND | Some Testimonies by |
ERNEST HEMINGWAY | FORD MADOX FORD | T. S. ELIOT |
HUGH WALPOLE | ARCHIBALD MacLEISH | JAMES JOYCE |
and OTHERS | FARRAR & RINEHART, Inc. [*device*] PUBLISH-
ERS : NEW YORK

> 22, [2] pp. 20 × 13 cm. Unbound; stapled.
>     Issued early in 1933 in connexion with the publication, by the
> same firm, of Pound's *A Draft of XXX Cantos* (1933).
>     'From T. S. Eliot', dated December 1, 1932: pp. 16–17.

B27         THE COLLECTED POEMS         1933
                OF HAROLD MONRO

THE COLLECTED POEMS | of | HAROLD MONRO | edited by | | ALIDA MONRO | with | a biographical sketch by | F. S. FLINT | and | a critical note by | T. S. ELIOT | [*device*] | London | COBDEN-SANDERSON | mcmxxxiii

> xx, 217 pp., 1 blank leaf. front.(port.) $22\frac{1}{2} \times 15$ cm. 8s. 6d. Blue cloth lettered in gold on spine; end-papers. White dust-wrapper printed in black and blue.
>> Published in May 1933. *On verso of title-page*: First published 1933 'Critical [Note]': pp. xiii–xvi.

B28    'SHAKESPEARIAN CRITICISM:    1934
        I. FROM DRYDEN TO COLERIDGE'

A COMPANION TO | SHAKESPEARE STUDIES | Edited by | | HARLEY GRANVILLE-BARKER | AND | G. B. HARRISON | CAMBRIDGE | AT THE UNIVERSITY PRESS | 1934

> 1 blank leaf, x, 408 pp. illus.(incl. plans), facsims. $22 \times 15$ cm. 12s. 6d. Blue cloth stamped in blind on front cover and in gold on spine; end-papers. Blue dust-wrapper printed in black and red.
>> 5,000 copies were published in March 1934. The book was issued in New York by Macmillan on April 23, 1934.
>> Contains 'Shakespearian Criticism: I. From Dryden to Coleridge, by T. S. Eliot': pp. [287]–299.

B29         'THE STORY OF THE         1934
                PAGEANT'

MAY 28th—JUNE 9th, 1934. | [*Rule*] | SADLERS WELLS THEATRE | [*rule*] | [*design by Eric Newton*] | T | H | E | ROCK | [*rule*] | (Price 3d.)

> 20 pp. $24\frac{1}{2} \times 15\frac{1}{2}$ cm. 3d. Unbound; stapled.
>> Published on May 28, 1934, and sold at the performances of the play at Sadlers Wells. A slip concerning the Iconoclasm scene, measuring approximately $11 \times 14\frac{1}{2}$ cm., was loosely inserted in some copies.
>> Contains 'The Story of the Pageant', by T. S. Eliot and Martin Browne: p. 7.

B30 , 'WORDS FOR MUSIC' [1934]

The | BEST POEMS | of 1934 | [*device*] | Selected by | THOMAS
MOULT | & decorated by | MERLYN MANN | LONDON |
Jonathan Cape Limited | TORONTO

123, [1] pp. (incl. front.), 2 blank leaves. 19 × 13½ cm. *6s.* Grey
cloth stamped in red on front cover, with white paper label printed
in black on spine; decorated end-papers. Cream dust-wrapper
printed in red and black.

Published in September 1934. *On verso of title-page*: First published
1934. . . . Sheets for 1,040 copies were imported and published in
New York on November 8, 1934, by Harcourt, Brace.

Contains 'Words for Music ["New Hampshire", "Virginia"]',
by T. S. Eliot: p. 107.

B31 'RELIGION [1935]
AND LITERATURE'

FAITH THAT ILLUMINATES | Edited, with an Introduction | by
| V. A. DEMANT | [*device*] | THE CENTENARY PRESS | Two
Manchester Square, London, W.

192 pp. 19 × 13 cm. *3s. 6d.* Red cloth lettered in gold on spine.
Cream dust-wrapper printed in red and black.

*On verso of title-page*: First published in March 1935

Contains 'Religion and Literature, by T. S. Eliot': pp. [29]–54.

B32 SELECTED POEMS BY 1935
MARIANNE MOORE

*a. First edition:*

SELECTED POEMS | by | MARIANNE MOORE | with | an intro-
duction by | T. S. ELIOT | New York | THE MACMILLAN COM-
PANY | 1935

xvi pp., 1 leaf, 126 pp. 22½ × 15½ cm. $2.00. Green cloth stamped
in silver on front cover and on spine; end-papers. White dust-
wrapper printed in black.

Edited by T. S. Eliot. *On verso of title-page*: Published April [9],
1935.

*b. First English edition* ([1935]):

SELECTED POEMS | by | MARIANNE MOORE | with | an intro-
duction by | T. S. ELIOT | London | FABER AND FABER LIMITED
| 24 Russell Square

> 1 blank leaf, 142 pp. 22½ × 15½ cm. 7s. 6d. Red cloth lettered in gold
> on spine; end-papers. Violet dust-wrapper printed in black and red.
> 1,000 copies were published on April 11, 1935. *On verso of title-
> page*: First published in April MCMXXXV . . .

B33         'DIFFICULTIES         [1936]
             OF A STATESMAN'

THE FABER BOOK | OF MODERN VERSE | edited by | MICHAEL
| ROBERTS | London | FABER AND FABER | 24 Russell Square

> 1 blank leaf, 2 leaves, vii–xvi, 352 pp. 19½ × 13 cm. 7s. 6d. Blue
> cloth lettered in gold on spine; end-papers. Red dust-wrapper
> printed in black and blue.
> 5,080 copies were published on February 27, 1936. *On verso of
> title-page*: First published in February Mcmxxxvi . . .
> Contains 'Difficulties of a Statesman': pp. 123–5. The other
> selections from T. S. Eliot included in this anthology had already
> appeared elsewhere separately or in book-form.

B34       ['IN MEMORIAM']       [1936]

POEMS OF TENNYSON | With an Introduction by | T. S. ELIOT |
THOMAS NELSON AND SONS LTD | LONDON EDINBURGH
PARIS MELBOURNE | TORONTO AND NEW YORK

> xix, 482 pp., 5 leaves, incl. front.(port.) 16½ × 11 cm. (The Nelson
> Classics) 1s. 6d. (60c.). Blue cloth lettered in gold on spine; end-
> papers. White dust-wrapper printed in red and in colours with
> portrait of Tennyson.
> 2,780 copies were published in May 1936. An additional 750
> copies were issued simultaneously at 2s. 6d. ( $1.00) in green rexine
> stamped in gold on spine, with end-papers; cellophane dust-
> wrapper with grey paper flaps printed in black, and white paper
> wrap-around, with the price printed in blue; in a cardboard case.
> 'Introduction': pp. ix–xix. Reprinted as 'In Memoriam'.

B35          'A NOTE ON THE          1936
          VERSE OF JOHN MILTON'

ESSAYS AND STUDIES | BY MEMBERS OF | THE ENGLISH
ASSOCIATION | VOL. XXI | COLLECTED BY HERBERT READ |
OXFORD | AT THE CLARENDON PRESS | 1936

168 pp. 22 × 15 cm. 7s. 6d. Green cloth stamped in blind on front
and back covers and in gold on spine; end-papers. Grey dust-
wrapper printed in blue.
    1,500 copies were published on July 2, 1936.
    Contains 'A Note on the Verse of John Milton', by T. S. Eliot:
pp. [32]–40.


B36          'THE IDEALISM          [1936]
          OF JULIEN BENDA'

The | NEW REPUBLIC | Anthology | 1915 : 1935 | . | Edited by |
GROFF CONKLIN | Introduction by | BRUCE BLIVEN | [*device*] |
DODGE PUBLISHING COMPANY | New York [*all the above
within double-ruled border*]

xlii, 566 pp. 22 × 15½ cm. $3.00. Grey cloth lettered in red and black
on front cover and on spine; end-papers. White dust-wrapper
printed in cream, black, and red.
    Published on October 5, 1936. Approximately 2,000 bound copies
were sold, and there was a remainder of about 1,200 sets of sheets.
*On verso of title-page*: First edition
    Contains 'The Idealism of Julien Benda [by] T. S. Eliot, Decem-
ber 12, 1928': pp. 293–300.


B37          'THE CHURCH'S          [1936]
          MESSAGE TO THE WORLD'

CHURCH, COMMUNITY | AND STATE | SYNOPSES OF TALKS
| NATIONAL PROGRAMME | TUESDAYS 12 JANUARY TO
16 FEBRUARY 1937 | 9.20 TO 9.40 PM | BBC [London]

23, [1] pp. 21½ × 14 cm. 3d. White paper wrappers printed in black;
sewn.
    8,500 copies were published on December 7, 1936.
    Contains 'The Church's Message to the World [by] T. S. Eliot':
pp. 19–21. The complete text was printed in *The Listener* (February
17, 1937) and as an appendix to *The Idea of a Christian Society* (1939).

**B38**      'BYRON (1788–1824)'      [1937]

[*Ornamental head-piece*] | FROM | ANNE TO VICTORIA | Essays by various hands | Edited by | Bonamy Dobrée | [*device*] | CASSELL | and Company Limited | London, Toronto, Melbourne | and Sydney

    x, 630 pp. 22 × 15 cm. 10*s*. 6*d*. Red cloth stamped in gold on spine; end-papers. White dust-wrapper printed in colour and in black. Blue paper wrap-around printed in blue.

    5,000 copies were published on February 18, 1937. Publishers' note concerning the title, a slip approximately 10½ × 12½ cm., loosely laid in before the title-page. *On verso of title-page*: First published in 1937

    Contains 'Byron (1788–1824), by T. S. Eliot': pp. 601–19.


**B39**      NIGHTWOOD      [1937]

*a. First edition:*

Djuna Barnes | NIGHTWOOD | HARCOURT, BRACE AND COMPANY | NEW YORK

    xiv pp., 2 leaves, 3–211 pp., 2 blank leaves. 21 × 14½ cm. $2.50. Blue cloth lettered in gold on spine; end-papers. Grey dust-wrapper printed in black and red.

    2,000 copies were published on March 4, 1937. *On verso of title-page*: first American edition

    Contains 'Introduction': pp. vii–xiv. This Introduction (reprinted in England in *The Criterion*, April 1937) does not appear in the first (English) edition of *Nightwood*, and was published in book-form for the first time in England in the second (English) edition described below.

*b. Second (English) edition ([1950]):*

NIGHTWOOD | by | Djuna Barnes | with a preface by | T. S. ELIOT | Faber and Faber Ltd | 24 Russell Square | London

    1 blank leaf, 3 leaves, 239 pp. 21 × 14½ cm. 12*s*. 6*d*. Lavender cloth stamped in red and lettered in gold on spine; end-papers. Blue dust-wrapper printed in black.

    2,000 copies were published on May 19, 1950. *On verso of title-page*: First published in Mcmxxxvi . . . Second edition Mcml . . . This edition was published in the United States by New Directions, New York.

    'Introduction': pp. 1–7, and 'Note to Second Edition': p. 8, by T. S. Eliot.

B40        REVELATION        [1937]

REVELATION | by | GUSTAF AULÉN | KARL BARTH | SERGIUS BULGAKOFF | M. C. D'ARCY | T. S. ELIOT | WALTER M. HORTON | WILLIAM TEMPLE | edited by | JOHN BAILLIE | and | HUGH MARTIN | FABER AND FABER LIMITED | 24 Russell Square | London

    1 blank leaf, 2 leaves, vii–xxiv, 312 pp. $19\frac{1}{2} \times 13\frac{1}{2}$ cm. 7s. 6d. Blue cloth lettered in gold on spine; end-papers. Blue dust-wrapper printed in red and black.

    1,517 copies were published on June 3, 1937. *On verso of title-page*: First published in June Mcmxxxvii . . .

    '1. By T. S. Eliot': pp. 1–39.

B41        'POETRY AND        1937
PROPAGANDA'

LITERARY OPINION | IN AMERICA | Essays Illustrating the Status, Methods, | and Problems of Criticism in the | United States Since the War | EDITED, WITH AN INTRODUCTION BY | MORTON DAUWEN ZABEL | [*device*] | 1937 | HARPER & BROTHERS | NEW YORK LONDON

    2 leaves, iii–liv, 637 pp., 1 blank leaf. $22\frac{1}{2} \times 15$ cm. $3.25. Brown cloth stamped in gold on front cover and on spine; end-papers. Green dust-wrapper printed in brown.

    2,500 copies were published on September 8, 1937. *On verso of title-page*: First edition H-M [i.e. August, 1937]

    Contains 'Poetry and Propaganda': pp. 25–38. The two other essays by T. S. Eliot included in this collection had already appeared elsewhere in book-form.

    'Errata' slip tipped in following p. [638].

B42        AUTHORS TAKE        [1937]
SIDES ON THE SPANISH WAR

AUTHORS TAKE SIDES | ON THE SPANISH WAR | LEFT REVIEW | 2 Parton Street | London | W. C. 1

    [32] pp. $25 \times 15\frac{1}{2}$ cm. 6d. Yellow paper wrappers printed in red; stapled. Red paper wrap-around printed in black.

    Published in December 1937.

    Consists of answers to a questionnaire sent to various writers in June 1937. T. S. Eliot's brief reply appears under the heading 'Neutral?' on p. [29].

B43      'A NOTE ON TWO      1938
ODES OF COWLEY'

SEVENTEENTH CENTURY | STUDIES | PRESENTED TO |
SIR HERBERT GRIERSON | OXFORD | AT THE CLARENDON
PRESS | 1938

> xv,415,[1] pp. front.(port.) 23 × 15½ cm. 21*s*. Blue cloth stamped
> in gold on spine; end-papers. Grey dust-wrapper printed in blue.
> Edited by John Purves; published on January 13, 1938.
> Contains 'A Note on Two Odes of Cowley', by T. S. Eliot: pp.
> [235]–242.

B44      'LITERATURE AND THE      1938
MODERN WORLD'

AMERICA | THROUGH THE ESSAY | An Anthology for English
Courses | EDITED BY | A. THEODORE JOHNSON | Professor of
English | Southwestern at Memphis | AND | ALLEN TATE |
Professor of English | The Woman's College of the University of
North Carolina | New York | OXFORD UNIVERSITY PRESS |
1938

> 7 leaves, 3–500 pp. 22½ × 15 cm. $2.00. Red cloth lettered in gold
> on spine; end-papers. Glacine dust-wrapper.
> 3,125 copies were published on April 21, 1938.
> Contains 'Literature and the Modern World by T. S. Eliot':
> pp. 379–86.

B45      POETS AT PRAYER      1938

POETS | AT PRAYER | by | Sister Mary James Power, S.S.N.D. |
[*ornament*] | SHEED & WARD | NEW YORK and LONDON | 1938

> 1 blank leaf, xxxvi, 214 pp., 2 blank leaves. facsims. 22 × 14½ cm.
> $3.00. Brown or green cloth stamped in silver on spine; end-papers.
> Grey dust-wrapper printed in red and green.
> Published on December 5, 1938. *On verso of title-page*: First
> printing, November, 1938
> Contains a letter from T. S. Eliot, dated December 6, 1932, on
> p. [126], with a photograph of it on the opposite plate.

B46         NOCTES BINANIANÆ         1939

NOCTES | BINANIANÆ | Certain Voluntary and Satyrical | Verses and Compliments as were lately | Exchang'd between some | of the Choicest Wits of the Age | LONDON | Collected with the greatest care | and now printed without | castration after the most correct copies | MCMXXXIX [*all the above within double-rule border*]

> 3 leaves, 25, [1] pp. 24 × 15½ cm. Not for sale. Stiff brown paper wrappers lettered on front cover; sewn. 'Corrigenda fulicalia', slip tipped on to verso of title-page.
>
> *Colophon* (*p.* [26]): 25 copies printed No. . . . Printed by Lund Humphries & Co. Ltd., London and Bradford.
>
> Privately printed before August 15, 1939.
>
> This collection of light verse, written and exchanged by G. C. Faber, F. V. Morley, T. S. Eliot, and John Hayward was printed for their amusement at the charge of E. C. Gregory, chairman of Lund Humphries.
>
> Contains the following poems by T. S. Eliot, anonymously: 'How to Pick a Possum', pp. 1–2; 'The O'Possum Strikes Back', pp. 3–4; 'The Whale and the Elephant: A Fable', p. 4; 'Ode to a Roman Coot', pp. 10–12; 'Three Sonnets', pp. 14–16; 'Vers pour la Foulque; Feuillet d'Album' [in French], pp. 19–20; 'Translation into English of "Verses for the Coot", Album Leaflet', pp. 20–21; 'Abschied zur Bina' [in German], p. 23–25.

B47         THE QUEEN'S BOOK         [1939]
            OF THE RED CROSS

THE | QUEEN'S BOOK | OF THE | RED CROSS | [*ornament*] | With a Message from | HER MAJESTY THE QUEEN | and Contributions by | FIFTY BRITISH AUTHORS AND ARTISTS | In Aid of | THE LORD MAYOR OF LONDON'S FUND | FOR THE RED CROSS AND THE ORDER | OF ST. JOHN OF JERUSALEM | [*ornament*] | [London] HODDER AND STOUGHTON

> 255 pp. front.(port.), illus., plates (part col.), music, facsim. 5s. 25½ × 19½ cm. Blue cloth printed in red on front cover and on spine; end-papers. White dust-wrapper printed in blue, red, and black.
>
> Published on December 7, 1939, in a total edition (all bindings) of 200,000 copies. (Also issued at 10s. 6d. in a 'de luxe' binding of white buckram stamped in gold and red on front cover and on spine, with end-papers, glacine dust-wrapper, and white cardboard box stamped in red on cover; also at 2s. 6d. in white paper wrappers

folded over cardboard, printed in blue, red, and black. The wrappered copies are a full centimetre shorter each way than those in other bindings.) *On verso of title-page*: First printed. . . . November 1939. In the later copies the words 'Winston Churchill' are added at the bottom of the plate facing p. 160.

    Contains 'The Marching Song of the Pollicle Dogs', and 'Billy M'Caw: The Remarkable Parrot', by T. S. Eliot: pp. 51–54.

B48          THE TESTAMENT OF      [1940]
## IMMORTALITY

THE TESTAMENT OF | IMMORTALITY | an anthology | selected and arranged by | N. G[angulee]. | with a preface by | T. S. ELIOT | [*quotation in five lines*] | FABER AND FABER LIMITED | 24 Russell Square | London

    280 pp. 19½ × 13½ cm. 8s. 6d. Blue cloth lettered in gold on spine; end-papers. Cream dust-wrapper printed in blue and black.

    2,000 copies were published on September 26, 1940. *On verso of title-page*: First published in September Mcmxl . . .

    'Preface by T. S. Eliot': pp. 9–10.

B49            IRVING BABBITT          1941

IRVING BABBITT | MAN AND TEACHER | Edited by | FREDERICK MANCHESTER | ODELL SHEPARD | [*device in red*] | [*ornament*] | G · P · PUTNAM'S SONS · New York | 1941 [*all the above within border of a single and double rule*]

    xiii, 337 pp. front.(port.), plates, facsim. 22½ × 15½ cm. $3.00. Grey cloth stamped in blind on front cover and in gold on spine; end-papers. White dust-wrapper printed in red and black.

    1,000 copies were published on September 5, 1941.

    A series of independent memoirs. 'By T. S. Eliot': pp. 101–4.

B50          'TOWARDS A      [1941]
## CHRISTIAN BRITAIN'

THE CHURCH LOOKS | AHEAD | Broadcast Talks | by | J. H. OLDHAM | MAURICE B. RECKITT | PHILIP MAIRET | DOROTHY L. SAYERS | M. C. D'ARCY, S. J. | V. A. DEMANT | T. S. ELIOT | with a preface by | E. L. MASCALL | FABER AND FABER LTD | 24 Russell Square | London

    122 pp., 3 blank leaves. 19 × 13 cm. 3s. 6d. Blue cloth lettered in

black on spine; end-papers. Buff dust-wrapper printed in black and red.

3,020 copies were published on November 13, 1941. *On verso of title-page*: First published in November Mcmxli . . .

'Towards a Christian Britain, by T. S. Eliot': pp. 106–17.


B51                A CHOICE OF                [1941]
                KIPLING'S VERSE

*a. First edition:*

A Choice of | KIPLING'S VERSE | made by | T. S. ELIOT | with an essay on | RUDYARD KIPLING | FABER AND FABER LTD | 24 Russell Square | London

306 pp., 1 blank leaf. $20\frac{1}{2} \times 14$ cm. 8s. 6d. Blue cloth lettered in gold on spine; end-papers. Blue dust-wrapper printed in black and red.

10,120 copies were published on December 11, 1941. *On verso of title-page*: First published in December Mcmxli . . .

*b. First American edition (1943):*

A Choice of | KIPLING'S VERSE | made by | T. S. ELIOT | with an essay on | RUDYARD KIPLING | New York | CHARLES SCRIBNER'S SONS | 1943

3 leaves, 5–306 pp., 2 blank leaves. $19\frac{1}{2} \times 14$ cm. $2.50. Green cloth lettered in gold on spine; end-papers. White dust-wrapper printed in green.

2,000 copies were published on August 9, 1943. *On verso of title-page*: A


B52            'THE CHRISTIAN            [1941]
        CONCEPTION OF EDUCATION'

MALVERN, 1941 | THE | LIFE OF THE CHURCH | AND THE | ORDER OF SOCIETY | BEING THE PROCEEDINGS OF | THE ARCHBISHOP OF YORK'S CONFERENCE | LONGMANS, GREEN AND CO. | LONDON : NEW YORK : TORONTO

xv, 235 pp. $22\frac{1}{2} \times 14\frac{1}{2}$ cm. 10s. 6d. Blue cloth lettered in black on spine; end-papers. Cream dust-wrapper printed in red.

Published in December 1941. *On verso of title-page*: First published 1941

Contains 'The Christian Conception of Education by T. S. Eliot': pp. 201–13.

B53     THE LITTLE BOOK OF     [1942]
MODERN VERSE

THE LITTLE BOOK | OF MODERN VERSE | chosen by | ANNE
RIDLER | with a preface by | T. S. ELIOT | FABER AND FABER |
24 Russell Square | London

160 pp. 19½ × 13 cm. *3s. 6d.* Tan cloth lettered downward in black
on spine; end-papers. Blue dust-wrapper printed in green and black
with title: A Little Book of Modern Verse with an Introduction by
T. S. Eliot, selected by Anne Ridler.

4,975 copies were published on February 5, 1942. *On verso of
title-page*: First published in November Mcmxli [*sic*] . . .

'Preface': pp. 5–9.

B54    INTRODUCING JAMES JOYCE [1942]

INTRODUCING | JAMES | JOYCE | a selection of Joyce's prose |
by | T. S. ELIOT | with | an introductory note | FABER AND FABER
LTD | 24 Russell Square | London

146 pp., 1 blank leaf. 19 × 13 cm. (Sesame Books) *3s. 6d.* Yellow
cloth lettered in brown on spine; end-papers. Yellow dust-wrapper
lettered in brown.

5,000 copies were published on October 23, 1942. *On verso of
title-page*: First published in September [*sic*] Mcmxlii. . . . This book
has not been published in the United States.

A slip headed 'Acknowledgment' is tipped in after p. [8] in the
later copies of the first impression.

B55     'A NOTE ON     1942
WAR POETRY'

LONDON | CALLING | EDITED BY | Storm Jameson | [*device*] |
HARPER & BROTHERS · PUBLISHERS | New York and London |
1942

vi pp., 1 leaf, 322 pp., 1 leaf, 2 blank leaves. 21½ × 15 cm. $2.50.
Brown cloth stamped in blind on front cover and in grey and gold
on spine; end-papers. White dust-wrapper printed in tan, green,
and black.

2,000 copies were published on November 13, 1942. *On verso of
title-page*: First edition K-R

Contains 'A Note on War Poetry [by] T. S. Eliot': pp. 237–8.

B56 [LETTER TO [1943]
HALLIE FLANAGAN]

DYNAMO | [*quotation in nine lines*] | HALLIE FLANAGAN |
DUELL, SLOAN AND PEARCE | NEW YORK

> 6 leaves, 3–176 pp., 1 blank leaf. 8 plates. 23½ × 16 cm. $2.75. Red
> buckram lettered in silver downward on spine; end-papers.
>> Published on May 21, 1943.
>> Contains a letter from T. S. Eliot, dated March 18, 1933, on
>> pp. 82–84. This concerns the production by the Vassar Experi-
>> mental Theatre, Poughkeepsie, New York, on May 6, 1933, of
>> *Sweeney Agonistes* as part of a mime sequence entitled 'Now I know
>> Love', and includes an additional short concluding scene for the
>> play. This scene was used in the Vassar production but has not been
>> incorporated in subsequent editions of the text.

B57 'HENRY JAMES' 1943

THE SHOCK | OF | RECOGNITION | [*ornament*] | THE DEVELOP-
MENT OF LITERATURE | IN THE UNITED STATES | RE-
CORDED BY THE MEN | WHO MADE IT | EDITED BY |
EDMUND WILSON | [*illustration*] | DOUBLEDAY, DORAN AND
COMPANY, INC. | GARDEN CITY NEW YORK | 1943

> 1 blank leaf, xv pp., 1 leaf, 1,290 pp., 1 blank leaf. 20 × 12 cm. $5.00.
> Blue cloth stamped in blind on front cover and lettered in gold on
> spine; cream end-papers. Cream dust-wrapper printed in grey and
> black.
>> Published on June 4, 1943. *On verso of title-page*: CL . . . First
>> edition
>> Contains 'Henry James I. In Memory [and II. The Hawthorne
>> Aspect]', by T. S. Eliot: pp. 854–65, reprinted from *The Little
>> Review*, January and August 1918. These essays were reprinted in
>> England as 'On Henry James' in *The Question of Henry James, A
>> Collection of Critical Essays; edited by F. W. Dupee* (London, Allan
>> Wingate [1947]), pp. 123–33.

B58 'TO THE INDIANS [1943]
WHO DIED IN AFRICA'

Queen Mary's | Book | FOR INDIA | [*device*] | WITH A FORE-
WORD BY | THE RIGHT HON. L. S. AMERY M. P. | GEORGE
G. HARRAP & CO. LTD. | LONDON TORONTO BOMBAY
SYDNEY

102, [1] pp. front.(port.), plates, facsims. $20\frac{1}{2} \times 14$ cm. 7s. 6d.
Blue cloth lettered downward in gold on spine; end-papers. White
dust-wrapper printed in blue, brown, and black.

5,000 copies were published on July 22, 1943. *On verso of title-
page*: First published 1943

Contains 'To the Indians who died in Africa, by T. S. Eliot':
p. 61, with a facsimile of his signature. Reprinted, with slight changes
in punctuation and omission of the third stanza, in *The Tiger
Triumphs: The Story of Three Great Divisions in Italy* ([London]
H.M. Stationery Office for the Government of India, 1946), p. [iii].

B59        'CIVILISATION:        [1943]
## THE NATURE OF
## CULTURAL RELATIONS'

FRIENDSHIP | PROGRESS | CIVILISATION | Three War-time
Speeches to | the Anglo-Swedish Society by | The Rt. Hon. LORD
SEMPILL, A.F.C. | The Hon. HAROLD NICOLSON, C.M.G.,
M.P. | Mr. T. S. ELIOT | [*device*] | PUBLISHED BY THE ANGLO-
SWEDISH SOCIETY | STAPLE INN, HIGH HOLBORN, W.C.1 |
Price One Shilling [*all the above within ornamental type border*]

cover-title, 23, [1] pp. $20\frac{1}{2} \times 13$ cm. 1s. Blue paper wrappers printed
in black; stapled.

3,000 copies were published in the autumn of 1943.

'Civilisation: The Nature of Cultural Relations, by T. S. Eliot':
pp. 15–20. A speech made at the Anglo-Swedish Society luncheon
on March 18, 1943.

B60        SHAKESPEARE &        [1943]
## THE POPULAR DRAMATIC TRADITION

SHAKESPEARE & | THE POPULAR | DRAMATIC TRADITION
| BY S. L. BETHELL, M. A., Cantab. | Lecturer in English Language
and Literature in the | University College of South Wales and
Monmouthshire | With an Introduction by | T. S. Eliot | [*device*] |
P. S. KING AND STAPLES LIMITED | A Staples Press Company |
14 GREAT SMITH STREET, WESTMINSTER, SW I

164 pp. front. $22 \times 14$ cm. Brown cloth lettered upward in brown on
spine; end-papers. Cream dust-wrapper printed in brown.

Issued in June 1944. *On verso of title-page*: First published 1944.
An American edition was published at Durham, North Carolina, by
the Duke University Press, on February 26, 1945.

'Introduction': pp. [7–9].

B61         INOUBLIABLE  FRANCE         [1944]

INOUBLIABLE FRANCE | ALICE JAHIER | Introduit par | T. S.
ELIOT | Avec quarante-deux photographies | SYLVAN PRESS ·
NICHOLSON & WATSON

[93] pp., 1 blank leaf. illus. $28\frac{1}{2} \times 22\frac{1}{2}$ cm. 15s. Grey cloth lettered in
blue on front cover and upward on spine; end-papers. Grey dust-
wrapper lettered in black and blue.
   *Title also in English on p.* [2]: France Remembered, translated by
J. G. Weightman, Introduction by T. S. Eliot; with forty-two
photographs.
   5,000 copies were published on July 26, 1944. *On verso of title-
page*: First impression made and printed in Great Britain by Page &
Thomas Ltd., Chesham June 1944
   'To the Reader', by T. S. Eliot, with translation 'Au Lecteur': p. [5].


B62         'CULTURAL  FORCES         [1945]
          IN  THE  HUMAN  ORDER'

PROSPECT | FOR CHRISTENDOM | [*ornament*] | Essays in |
Catholic Social Reconstruction | edited by | MAURICE B. RECKITT
| FABER AND FABER LIMITED | 24 Russell Square | London

255 pp. $22\frac{1}{2} \times 14\frac{1}{2}$ cm. 12s. 6d. Blue cloth lettered in gold on spine;
end-papers. White dust-wrapper printed in red and black.
   1,000 copies were published on May 1, 1945. *On verso of title-
page*: First published in Mcmxlv . . .
   Contains 'Cultural Forces in the Human Order, by T. S. Eliot':
pp. 57–69. Reprinted and revised as Chapter I of *Notes towards the
Definition of Culture* (1948).


B63         '[A LETTER] FROM         [1945]
          T. S. ELIOT'

[*In black:*] THE CRACK-UP | F. SCOTT FITZGERALD | [*in
brown:*] With other uncollected pieces, | Note-Books and Unpublished
Letters | Together with letters to Fitz- | gerald from Gertrude Stein,
Edith | Wharton, T. S. Eliot, Thomas Wolfe | and John Dos Passos |
And essays and poems by paul | Rosenfeld, Glenway Wescott, John |
Dos Passos, John Peale Bishop and | Edmund Wilson | [*in black:*]
Edited by EDMUND WILSON | [*device in brown*] | [*in black:*] A
New Directions Book [New York, James Laughlin]

1 blank leaf, 347, [1] pp., 1 blank leaf. $24 \times 15$ cm. $3.50. Decorated

paper-covered boards, brown buckram back with brown label printed in black and brown; end-papers. Brown dust-wrapper printed in brown and black.

*Colophon* (*p.* [348]): . . . printed . . . by Peter Beilenson, Mount Vernon, N.Y. . . .

2,700 copies were published on August 12, 1945. Later impressions have title-page in black, are bound in tan cloth, and have no colophon.

'From T. S. Eliot', a letter dated December 31, 1925: p. 310. Reprinted as 'A Letter on The Great Gatsby' in *F. Scott Fitzgerald: The Man and his Work, edited by Alfred Kazin* (Cleveland, New York, World Publishing Company [1951]), pp. 93–94.

B64        THE DARK SIDE OF        [1946]
                    THE MOON

THE DARK SIDE | OF | THE MOON | with a preface by | T. S. ELIOT | FABER AND FABER LIMITED | 24 Russell Square | London

232 pp. $20\frac{1}{2} \times 14$ cm. 12s. 6d. Blue cloth lettered in gold on spine; end-papers. White dust-wrapper printed in red and grey.

8,366 copies were published on June 10, 1946. *On verso of title-page*: First published in Mcmxlvi. . . . An American edition was published in New York by Scribner's on February 24, 1947.

'Preface': pp. 5–8.

B65        'LEÇON DE VALÉRY'        1946

PAUL VALÉRY | vivant | [*device*] | [Marseille] CAHIERS DU SUD | MCMXLVI

1 blank leaf, 2 leaves, [7]–381, [1] pp., 1 leaf. front.(port.), plates. $22\frac{1}{2} \times 14$ cm. 320 fr. Grey paper wrappers folded over white paper, printed in red and blue.

*Colophon* (*p.* [382]): L'édition originale du présent ouvrage est constituée par les tirages suivants: quinze exemplaires sur japon des Papeteries Barjon, lettrés de A à O; quarante exemplaires sur vélin pur fil Lafuma, dont vingt-cinq numérotés de I à XXV et quinze marqués HC; cinq cents exemplaires sur vélin parcheminé, dont quatre cents numérotés de I à 400 et cent réservés aux collaborateurs de l'ouvrage et amis des Cahiers du Sud et qui paraîtront imprimés à leur nom.

*Colophon* (*p.* [383]): Achevé d'imprimer sur les presses de la Société du Petit Marseillais, le trente juillet mil neuf cent quarante-six, à Marseille . . . No d'édition 1

Contains 'T. S. Eliot Leçon de Valéry': pp. [74]–81. The English text and a French translation of it by Henri Fluchère are printed on opposite pages.

## B66 'TO WALTER DE LA MARE' [1948]

TRIBUTE TO | WALTER DE LA MARE | on his | Seventy-fifth Birthday | [*ornament*] | FABER AND FABER LIMITED | 24 Russell Square | London

195 pp. col. front., plate, 3 ports., fold. facsim. $22\frac{1}{2} \times 15$ cm. 15s. Blue buckram stamped in blind on front cover and in gold and rose on spine; end-papers. White dust-wrapper printed in red, blue, and black.

1,020 copies were published on April 23, 1948. *On verso of title-page*: First published in mcmxlviii . . .

Contains 'To Walter de la Mare', a poem, by T. S. Eliot: pp. 106–7.

## B67 JAMES JOYCE [1948]

james joyce: | two decades of criticism | BY: Eugene Jolas, Frank Budgen, Irene Hendry, Richard Levin, | Charles Shattuck, James T. Farrell, Hugh Kenner, T. S. Eliot, | S. Foster Damon, Philip Toynbee, Vivian Mercier, William Troy, | Edmund Wilson, Joseph Campbell, Frederick J. Hoffman, J. F. | Hendry, Stuart Gilbert. | EDITED BY SEON GIVENS · VANGUARD PRESS, INC., NEW YORK

3 blank leaves, xiii, [1], 3–482 pp., 2 blank leaves, incl. front. (port.), 1 illus. $24\frac{1}{2} \times 17$ cm. $5.00. Green cloth lettered in black on spine; end-papers. White dust-wrapper printed in black, with plan of Dublin in green.

Pages [i–iv] are printed on coated paper.

4,250 copies were published on July 12, 1948.

'T. S. Eliot. Ulysses, Order, and Myth', pp. 198–202, reprinted from *The Dial*, November 1923; 'T. S. Eliot. A Message to the Fish', pp. 468–71, reprinted from *Horizon*, March 1941.

## B68 ALL HALLOWS' EVE [1948]

Charles Williams | [*rule*] | ALL | HALLOWS' EVE | Introduction by T. S. Eliot | Pellegrini & Cudahy : New York

xviii pp., 1 leaf, 273 pp., 1 blank leaf. $21 \times 14\frac{1}{2}$ cm. $2.75. Blue cloth

lettered in gold on front cover and on spine; end-papers. White
dust-wrapper printed in plum and black.

    3,500 copies were published on October 18, 1948.

    'Introduction': pp. ix–xviii. This is a revised version of 'The
Significance of Charles Williams', printed from the broadcast text
in *The Listener*, December 19, 1946.


B69          EN ENGELSK BOG          1948

[*In red:*] En engelsk Bog | [*in black:*] Tilegnet | Kai Friis Møller |
KØBENHAVN | [*short rule in red*] | [*in black:*] Gyldendalske Boghandel
| 1948

    1 blank leaf, 5 leaves, 9–182, [1] pp., 1 leaf, 1 blank leaf. 20½ × 14
cm. Kr. 20. White paper wrappers lettered in red and black on front
cover, in red on spine, and in black on back cover. Glacine dust-
wrapper.

    750 copies printed December 15, 1948, with one copy on special
paper for Kai Friis Møller.

    Contains 'Introduction' [in English], by T. S. Eliot: p. [7].


B70        'BALLADE OF THE        1949
              FOX DINNER'

FIFTY YEARS | William R. Castle, 'OO | [*device*] | [Cambridge,
Mass.] Printed Privately for the Fox Club | 1949

    2 leaves, 22 pp., 1 blank leaf. 19 × 12½ cm. Not for sale. Stiff
green paper wrappers printed in gold on front cover; stapled.

    1,000 copies were distributed to members in the spring of 1949.

    Contains 'Ballade of the Fox Dinner by T. S. Eliot, '10': pp.
12–13, verses read on May 15, 1909.


B71        'THE SOCIAL        [1949]
      FUNCTION OF POETRY'

CRITIQUES | and | ESSAYS IN CRITICISM | 1920–1948 | RE-
PRESENTING THE ACHIEVEMENT OF MODERN | BRITISH
AND AMERICAN CRITICS | Selected By | ROBERT WOOSTER
STALLMAN | UNIVERSITY OF KANSAS | WITH A FORE-
WORD BY | CLEANTH BROOKS | THE RONALD PRESS
COMPANY [*ornament*] NEW YORK

1 blank leaf, xxii, 571 pp., 2 blank leaves. 24 × 16½ cm. $5.00. Grey cloth stamped on front cover and on spine in red; white end-papers. Grey dust-wrapper printed in red.

3,000 copies were published on January 11, 1949.

Contains 'The Social Function of Poetry', by T. S. Eliot: pp. 105–16, reprinted from *The Adelphi*, July/September 1945.


B72 JAMES JOYCE 1949

JAMES JOYCE | SA VIE | SON ŒUVRE | SON RAYONNEMENT | OCTOBRE-NOVEMBRE | 1949 | LA HUNE | 170, BOULEVARD SAINT-GERMAIN | PARIS-VIᵉ

63 leaves, 1 blank leaf, incl. plates, ports., facsims. 21 × 16½ cm. 400 fr. ($1.35) Green paper wrappers printed in blue and black on both covers, flaps, and spine.

Title printed across two pages with only the word 'James' on the first.

*Colophon* (*p.* [126]): Le présent volume a été tiré à 1.500 exemplaires . . . les exemplaires 1 à 30 étant seuls numérotés. Ceux-ci comportent en hors-texte une eau-forte en deux tons de Johny Friedlander qui reproduit les armes de la famille Joyce.

Contains a prefatory note by T. S. Eliot on recto of the sixth leaf, and in French translation on verso of the fifth leaf. This note was reprinted in the catalogue of the Joyce Exhibition at the Institute of Contemporary Arts, London.


B73 [LETTER TO MARIO PRAZ] [1949]

T. S. ELIOT | LA TERRA DESOLATA | FRAMMENTO DI UN AGONE | MARCIA TRIONFALE | [*device*] | FUSSI | [*short rule*] | FIRENZE

1 blank leaf, 3 leaves, 9–91 pp., 2 leaves. 1 plate. 17 × 12 cm. 400 lire. (Il Melagrano, 40–41.) White paper wrappers printed in brown on covers and on spine.

*On verso of Italian title-page*: Edizione numerata di 2000 esemplari. [*Number of copy stamped in.*]

Title-page and text also in English, printed on opposite pages; translated by Mario Praz.

Contains 'Autografo da Lettura di T. S. Eliot al Traduttore': plate tipped in before p. 9. The letter is dated December 13, 1933, and is in English, without translation.

B74 A PORTRAIT 1949
OF MICHAEL ROBERTS

A PORTRAIT OF | MICHAEL ROBERTS | Edited by | T. W.
EASON and R. HAMILTON | COLLEGE OF S. MARK & S. JOHN
| CHELSEA | 1949

1 blank leaf, xii, 72 pp., 1 blank leaf.   front.(port.) plate. illus.
(facsim.) 22 × 14 cm. 4s. Grey paper wrappers printed in black on
front cover.

800 copies were privately printed on December 12, 1949.
Contains 'Introduction', by T. S. Eliot: pp. x–xii. This is a
slightly altered version of an obituary article published in *The New
English Weekly*, January 13, 1949.

B75 'THE POETRY OF 1950
W. B. YEATS'

The Permanence of | YEATS | SELECTED CRITICISM | Edited |
by | JAMES HALL | and | MARTIN STEINMANN | New York |
THE MACMILLAN COMPANY | 1950

vi pp., 2 leaves, 414 pp. 21½ × 14½ cm. $5.00. Blue cloth stamped in
gold on spine; end-papers. White dust-wrapper printed in green.
3,400 copies were published on January 31, 1950. *On verso of
title-page*: First printing
Contains 'The Poetry of W. B. Yeats', by T. S. Eliot: pp. 331–
43, reprinted from *The Southern Review*, Winter 1941, where it
was in turn reprinted from *Purpose*, July/December 1940.

B76 HALI [1950]

HALI | By G. V. Desani | [*rule*] | Foreword by T. S. Eliot & E. M.
Forster | Frontispiece: Sárika Góth | THE SATURN PRESS

1 blank leaf, 6 leaves, 17–57 pp.   col. front.(port.) 21½ × 14 cm.
7s. 6d. Red cloth stamped in gold on front cover; maroon imitation
leather back lettered upward in gold; maroon end-papers. White
dust-wrapper printed in red and black, with portrait in colour.
2,500 copies were published on February 10, 1950. *On verso of
title-page*: First published 1950 . . .
'Foreword': recto of fourth leaf. This is merely an extract from
a letter which was not intended for publication.

B77 [1950]
## LES PRIX NOBEL

LES PRIX NOBEL | EN 1948 | STOCKHOLM | IMPRIMERIE
ROYALE, P. A. NORSTEDT & SÖNER | 1949 [*i.e.* 1950]

132 pp. illus., diagrs., 4 plates (ports.) 25 × 17 cm. Stiff white paper
wrappers printed in red. (Copies for presentation to recipients of
prizes were in blue cloth lettered in gold, with paper wrappers
bound in.)

1,150 copies were published on February 27, 1950.

Contains T. S. Eliot's response to the toast at the Nobel Banquet
in Stockholm, December 10, 1948, pp. 56–58.

B78 ENGLISH POETRY [1950]

ENGLISH POETRY | and | its contribution to the knowledge | of a
creative principle | by | LEONE VIVANTE | with a preface by |
T. S. ELIOT | FABER AND FABER | 24 Russell Square | London

xv, 340 pp. 22½ × 15 cm. 21*s*. Blue cloth stamped in gold on spine;
end-papers. Lavender dust-wrapper printed in black and red.

1,780 copies were published on July 14, 1950. *On verso of title-
page*: First published in mcml. . . . Issued in New York, with a cancel
title-page, early in 1951 by Macmillan.

'Preface': pp. vii–xi.

B79 THE ADVENTURES 1950
OF HUCKLEBERRY FINN

THE | ADVENTURES | OF | HUCKLEBERRY FINN | by |
SAMUEL L. CLEMENS | (MARK TWAIN) | [*ornament*] | With
an Introduction by | T. S. ELIOT | [*ornament*] | LONDON | THE
CRESSET PRESS | MCML

1 blank leaf, xvi pp., 1 leaf, 291, [1] pp. 20 × 14 cm. 9*s. 6d.* (raised
to 10*s. 6d.* and then to 12*s. 6d.*). (The Cresset Library.) Blue
buckram stamped in gold on front cover and on spine; end-papers.
White dust-wrapper printed in tan, red, and black.

8,500 copies were published on September 25, 1950. Bound copies
were imported and published in New York in October 1950, by the
Chanticleer Press, whose imprint appears on the title-page, spine,
and dust-wrapper. *On verso of title-page*: Published in 1950 . . .

'Introduction': pp. vii–xvi.

B80 'EZRA POUND' [1950]

EZRA POUND | A collection of essays edited by | Peter Russell to be presented | to Ezra Pound on his sixty-fifth | birthday | PETER NEVILL LIMITED | London  New York

> 268 pp. front.(port.) $22 \times 14\frac{1}{2}$ cm. Tan cloth stamped in blue and gold on spine; end-papers. Cream dust-wrapper printed in blue and black.
>
> 2,000 copies were published on October 16, 1950. *On verso of title-page*: Made and printed in . . . MCML. Sheets for an additional 1,500 copies were imported and published in New York by New Directions under the title, *An Examination of Ezra Pound: A Collection of Essays edited by Peter Russell.*
>
> Contains 'Ezra Pound by T. S. Eliot ⟨1946⟩': pp. 25–35, with a 'Postscript, 1950': p. 36.

B81 THE LETTERS OF [1950]
EZRA POUND

THE LETTERS OF | EZRA POUND | 1907–1941 | EDITED BY D. D. PAIGE | [*quotation in one line*] | HARCOURT, BRACE AND COMPANY : NEW YORK

> xxv, 358 pp. $24\frac{1}{2} \times 16\frac{1}{2}$ cm. $5.00. Brown cloth stamped in blind on front cover and in gold on spine; end-papers. Yellow dust-wrapper printed in brown and red.
>
> 4,000 copies were published on October 26, 1950. *On verso of title-page*: first edition
>
> Contains a letter from T. S. Eliot to Ezra Pound, dated [? January 1922]: pp. 170–71. This letter was included (pp. 11–12) in an advertising leaflet distributed by the publishers in an edition of 15,000 copies shortly before publication of the book. The book was issued in England by Faber and Faber in 1951 at 25s.

B82 'GENTLEMEN AND SEAMEN' [1951]

The | HARVARD | ADVOCATE | Anthology | Edited by DONALD HALL | [*quotation in five lines between two rows of ornaments*] | TWAYNE PUBLISHERS, INC. · NEW YORK

> 327 pp. 4 plates. $23\frac{1}{2} \times 16$ cm. $5.00. Red cloth stamped in gold on front cover and on spine; end-papers. Grey dust-wrapper printed in dark grey and red.
>
> 4,200 copies were published on January 22, 1951.

Contains 'Gentlemen and Seamen' (prose): pp. 109–12, reprinted from the *Advocate*, May 25, 1909. Eight of the poems originally contributed by T. S. Eliot to the *Advocate* are also reprinted here, but none of them for the first time in book-form.

## B83       D. H. LAWRENCE AND       [1951] HUMAN EXISTENCE

D. H. LAWRENCE | and Human Existence | by | Father William Tiverton | FOREWORD BY | T. S. ELIOT | ROCKLIFF [*within device*] | SALISBURY SQUARE | LONDON

xv, 140 pp.    front.(port.)  22½ × 14½ cm.  12s. 6d. Orange cloth stamped in gold on spine; end-papers. White dust-wrapper printed in red.

2,500 copies were published on February 16, 1951. Of these 500 bound copies were imported and published in New York in May 1951, by the Philosophical Library, whose imprint appears on the title-page, spine, and dust-wrapper. *On verso of title-page*: First published 1951 . . .

'Foreword': pp. vii–[viii].

## B84        THOUGHTS FOR        [1951] MEDITATION

Thoughts for Meditation | A Way to Recovery from Within | * | an anthology | selected and arranged by | N. GANGULEE | with a preface by | T. S. ELIOT | [*quotation in three lines*] | * | FABER AND FABER LIMITED | 24 Russell Square | London

1 blank leaf, 3 leaves, 9–163 pp.  19½ × 13 cm.  9s. 6d. Blue cloth stamped in gold on spine; end-papers. Blue dust-wrapper printed in black and red.

3,045 copies were published on March 9, 1951. *On verso of title-page*: First published in mcmli . . .

'Preface': pp. 11–14.

## B85        'THE SPOKEN WORD'        1951

Festival of Britain 1951 | LONDON | SEASON OF THE | ARTS | May 1951 June [*the year 1951 is printed within an oval design of leaves*] | OFFICIAL SOUVENIR PROGRAMME | PUBLISHED FOR THE ARTS COUNCIL OF GREAT BRITAIN | BY LUND HUMPHRIES & CO LTD

96 pp. illus., 4 plates. 25 × 18½ cm. 2s. 6d. White paper wrappers printed in red and black; stapled.

Published in April 1951.

Contains 'The Spoken Word [by] T. S. Eliot, O.M.': pp. 6–9.

B86  MURDER IN THE  1951
CATHEDRAL, A SCREENPLAY

[*In black:*] T. S. ELIOT | [*in red:*] MURDER | IN THE | CATHE-DRAL | [*in black:*] A SCREENPLAY | GREAT BRITAIN [London, Film Traders Ltd] | MCMLI

cover-title, 16 pp. 2 leaves of illustrations, printed on both sides, stapled between p. 8 and p. 9. 25 × 19 cm. Not for sale. Stiff grey paper wrappers printed on front and back covers in black and red; stapled.

Pages 1–4, 13–16 printed on grey paper, pages 5–6, 11–12 on blue, and pages 7–10 on green. 'Erratum' slip tipped in before page 1.

Contains 'Preface', by T. S. Eliot, in English on p. 1, Italian on p. [2], French on p. 9, and German on p. 10, with 'Synopsis' in English on pp. 5–6, Italian on pp. 7–8, French on pp. 13–14, and German on pp. 15–16.

1,000 copies were printed and delivered on July 28, 1951, and were distributed for publicity purposes in Venice in connexion with the first showing of the film there at the International Film Festival in September 1951.

# C

---

## CONTRIBUTIONS BY
## T. S. ELIOT TO
## PERIODICALS[1]

[1] *Arranged chronologically. Contributions to a particular periodical are listed by reference number under the periodical in the Index of titles.*

*Titles of poems are printed in small capital letters.*

*The following abbreviations are used: IJE* (International Journal of Ethics); *TLS* (Times Literary Supplement, London), *and NEW* (New English Weekly).

# C. *Contributions to Periodicals*

NOTE: Mr. Eliot was one of the editors of *The Harvard Advocate*, 1909–10; assistant editor of *The Egoist*, 1917–19; editor of *The Criterion*, 1922–39, and has been at various times a member of the editorial boards of *The New English Weekly, The Christian News-Letter, Inventario*, and other periodicals.

C1. A FABLE FOR FEASTERS. *Smith Academy Record*, VIII. 2 (Feb. 1905) [1]–3.

C2. A LYRIC. *Smith Academy Record*, VIII. 4 (Apr. 1905) 3.
   Reprinted, with slight alterations, as 'Song' in *Harvard Advocate*, LXXXIII. 7 (June 3, 1907) 96.

C3. A Tale of a Whale. *Smith Academy Record*, VIII. 4 (Apr. 1905) [1]–3.

C4. The Man who was King. *Smith Academy Record*, VIII. 6 (June 1905) [1]–3.

C5. SONG ['When we came home across the hill']. *Harvard Advocate*, LXXXIII. 6 (May 24, 1907) 93.

C6. BEFORE MORNING. *Harvard Advocate*, LXXXVI. 4 (Nov. 13, 1908) 53.

C7. CIRCE'S PALACE. *Harvard Advocate*, LXXXVI. 5 (Nov. 25, 1908) 66.

C8. ON A PORTRAIT. *Harvard Advocate*, LXXXVI. 9 (Jan. 26, 1909) 135.

C9. SONG ['The moonflower opens to the moth']. *Harvard Advocate*, LXXXVI. 9 (Jan. 26, 1909) 130.

C10. [*A review of*] The Wine of the Puritans. [By] Van Wyck Brooks. *Harvard Advocate*, LXXXVII. 5 (May 7, 1909) [80].

C11. The Point of View. [An Editorial]. *Harvard Advocate*, LXXXVII. 6 (May 20, 1909) 82.
   Unsigned, but ascribed to T. S. Eliot in the index.

C12. Gentlemen and Seamen. *Harvard Advocate*, LXXXVII. 7 (May 25, 1909) 115–16.

C13. [*A review of*] Egoists. By James Huneker. *Harvard Advocate*, LXXXVIII. 1 (Oct. 5, 1909) 16.

C14. NOCTURNE. *Harvard Advocate*, LXXXVIII. 3 (Nov. 12, 1909) 39.

C15. HUMOURESQUE. (AFTER J. LAFORGUE). *Harvard Advocate*, LXXXVIII. 7 (Jan. 12, 1910) [103].

C16. SPLEEN. *Harvard Advocate*, LXXXVIII. 8 (Jan. 26, 1910) 114.

# C. *Contributions to Periodicals*

C17. [CLASS] ODE. *Harvard Advocate*, LXXXIX. 8 (June 24, 1910) [100].
Reprinted on the same day in the Boston *Evening Transcript* and the Boston *Evening Herald*.

C18. THE LOVE SONG OF J. ALFRED PRUFROCK. *Poetry*, VI. 3 (June 1915) 130–5.

C19. POEMS. *Blast*, 2 (July 1915) 48–51.
*Contents*: Preludes—Rhapsody of a Windy Night.

C20. PORTRAIT OF A LADY. *Others*, I. 3 (Sept. 1915) 35–40.
This poem was reprinted separately in 1941 by M. S. Howard on the Marlborough College Press in an edition of forty copies of which none was for sale.

C21. THREE POEMS. *Poetry*, VII. 1 (Oct. 1915) 21–22.
*Contents*: The Boston Evening Transcript—Aunt Helen—Cousin Nancy.
A fourth poem, 'The Death of Saint Narcissus', was set up in type apparently for publication in *Poetry*, but was not printed. Of it there exists, in the Harriet Monroe Collection at the University of Chicago, a cancelled galley proof, which provided the text printed in *Poems written in Early Youth* (1950).

C22. [*A review of*] Theism and Humanism. By the Rt. Hon. A. J. Balfour. *IJE*, XXVI. 2 (Jan. 1916) 284–9.

C23. Mr. Doughty's Epic. [*In an English periodical early in* 1916].
A review of *The Titans*, by Charles M. Doughty; signed: T.S.E.

C24. [*A review of*] The Philosophy of Nietzsche. By A. Wolf. *IJE*, XXVI. 3 (Apr. 1916) 426–7.

C25. An American Critic. *New Statesman*, VII. 168 (June 24, 1916) 284.
A review of *Aristocracy and Justice*, by Paul Elmer More. Reprinted as 'A Note on the American Critic'.

C26. [*A review of*] Group Theories of Religion and the Religion of the Individual. By Clement C. J. Webb. *New Statesman*, VII. 173 (July 29, 1916) 405–6.
Reprinted in *IJE*, XXVII. 1 (Oct. 1916) 115–17.

C27. [*A review of*] Social Adaptation, by L. M. Bristol. *New Statesman*, VII. 173 (July 29, 1916) 405.

C28. Mr. Leacock Serious. *New Statesman*, VII. 173 (July 29, 1916) 404–5.
A review of *Essays and Literary Studies*, by Stephen Leacock.

C29. OBSERVATIONS. *Poetry*, VIII. 6 (Sept. 1916) 292–5.
*Contents*: Conversation galante—La Figlia che Piange—Mr. Apollinax—Morning at the Window.

# C. *Contributions to Periodicals*

C30. [*A review of*] Conscience and Christ: Six Lectures on Christian Ethics. By Hastings Rashdall. *IJE*, XXVII. 1 (Oct. 1916) 111–12.

C31. The Development of Leibniz's Monadism. *Monist*, XXVI. 4 (Oct. 1916) [534]–556.

C32. Leibniz's Monads and Bradley's Finite Centers. *Monist*, XXVI. 4 (Oct. 1916) [566]–576.

C33. [*A review of*] The Ultimate Belief. By A. Clutton Brock. *IJE*, XXVII. 1 (Oct. 1916) 127.

C34. [*A review of*] Religion and Science: A Philosophical Essay. By John Theodore Merz. *IJE*, XXVII. 1 (Oct. 1916) 125–6.

C35. [*A review of*] Philosophy and War. By Émile Boutroux. *IJE*, XXVII. 1 (Oct. 1916) 128.

C36. Giordano Bruno. *New Statesman*, VIII. 185 (Oct. 21, 1916) 68.
A review of *Giordano Bruno: His Life, Thought, and Martyrdom*, by William Boulting.

C37. Classics in English. *Poetry*, IX. 2 (Nov. 1916) 101–4.
A review of *The Poets' Translation Series I–VI*.

C38. [*A review of*] Elements of Folk Psychology. Outlines of a Psychological History of the Development of Mankind. By Wilhelm Wundt. *IJE*, XXVII. 2 (Jan. 1917) 252–4.

C39. Reflections on *Vers Libre*. *New Statesman*, VIII. 204 (Mar. 3, 1917) 518–19.

C40. Eeldrop and Appleplex, I. *Little Review*, IV. 1 (May 1917) 7–11.
A pirated reprint appeared as 'Eeldrop and Appleplex, A Fragment' in Samuel Roth's *Two Worlds Monthly*, I. 2 (Sept. 1926) 189–92.

C41. The Borderline of Prose. *New Statesman*, IX. 215 (May 19, 1917) 157–9.

C42. [FOUR POEMS]. *Little Review*, IV. 3 (July 1917) 8–11.
*Contents*: Le Directeur—Mélange Adultère de Tout—Lune de Miel—The Hippopotamus.

C43. The Letters of J. B. Yeats. *Egoist*, IV. 6 (July 1917) 89–90.
A review of *Passages from the Letters of John Butler Yeats, selected by Ezra Pound*.

C44. [*A review of*] Mens Creatrix. By William Temple. *IJE*, XXVII. 4 (July 1917) 542–3.

C45. [*A review of*] Religion and Philosophy. By R. G. Collingwood. *IJE*, XXVII. 4 (July 1917) 543.

C46. The Noh and the Image. *Egoist*, IV. 7 (Aug. 1917) 102–3.
A review of *Noh, or Accomplishment, a Study of the Classical Stage of Japan*, by Ernest Fenollosa and Ezra Pound.

# C. *Contributions to Periodicals*

C47. Eeldrop and Appleplex. II. *Little Review*, IV. 5 (Sept. 1917) 16–19.

C48. Reflections on Contemporary Poetry. I. *Egoist*, IV. 8 (Sept. 1917) 118–19.

C49. Reflections on Contemporary Poetry. II. *Egoist*, IV. 9 (Oct. 1917) 133–4.

C50. [*A review of*] A Manual of Modern Scholastic Philosophy. By Cardinal Mercier and Other Professors of the Higher Institute of Philosophy, Louvain. . . . Vol. I. *IJE*, XXVIII. 1 (Oct. 1917) 137–8.

C51. Reflections on Contemporary Poetry. III. *Egoist*, IV. 10 (Nov. 1917) 151.

C52. Correspondence. *Egoist*, IV. 11 (Dec. 1917) 165.
    Extracts, actually composed by T. S. Eliot to fill up space, from letters purported to be written by J. A. D. Spence, Thridlingston Grammar School; Helen B. Trundlett, Batton, Kent; Charles James Grimble, The Vicarage, Leays; Charles Augustus Conybeare, The Carlton Club, Liverpool; and Muriel A. Schwarz, 60 Alexandra Gardens, Hampstead, N.W.

C53. Turgenev. *Egoist*, IV. 11 (Dec. 1917) 167.
    A review of *Turgenev*, by Edward Garnett, with a foreword by Joseph Conrad.

C54. Recent British Periodical Literature in Ethics. *IJE*, XXVIII. 2 (Jan. 1918) 270–7.

C55. In Memory of Henry James. *Egoist*, V. 1 (Jan. 1918) [1]–2.
    Reprinted as 'In Memory' in *Little Review*, V. 4 (Aug. 1918) 44–47.

C56. Literature and the American Courts. *Egoist*, V. 3 (Mar. 1918) 39.
    Concerns the suppression of a number of *The Little Review* which contained a story by Wyndham Lewis.

C57. Verse Pleasant and Unpleasant. *Egoist*, V. 3 (Mar. 1918) 43–44.
    Signed with the pseudonym, Apteryx. A review of *Georgian Poetry*, 1916–1917, edited by E. M[arsh]., and of *Wheels, A Second Cycle*.

C58. [A Letter]. To the Editor. *Egoist*, V. 3 (Mar. 1918) 47.

C59. Disjecta Membra. *Egoist*, V. 4 (Apr. 1918) 55.
    A review of *Tendencies in Modern American Poetry*, by Amy Lowell.

C60. [*A review of*] La Guerra Eterna e Il Dramma del Esistenza. By Antonio Aliotta. *IJE*, XXVIII. 3 (Apr. 1918) 444–5.

C61. [*A review of*] Brahmadarsanam, or Intuition of the Absolute.

## C. *Contributions to Periodicals*

Being an Introduction to the Study of Hindu Philosophy. By Sri
Ananda Acharya. *IJE*, xxviii. 3 (Apr. 1918) 445–6.

C62. Professional, or. . . . *Egoist*, v. 4 (Apr. 1918) 61.
Signed with the pseudonym, Apteryx.

C63. Observations. *Egoist*, v. 5 (May 1918) 69–70.
Signed with the pseudonym, T. S. Apteryx.

C64. Contemporanea. *Egoist*, v. 6 (June/July 1918) 84–85.

C65. [*A review of*] The World as Imagination. (Series I.) By Edward
Douglas Fawcett. *IJE*, xxviii. 4 (July 1918) 572.

C66. Short Notices. *Egoist*, v. 7 (Aug. 1918) 99.
A review of *In the Valley of Vision*, *Poems* by Geoffrey Faber;
*Sonnets and Poems*, by Eleanor Farjeon; *-Esques*, by E. F. A.
Geach and D. E. A. Wallace; *Resentment*, *Poems* by Alec Waugh.
The note on *Resentment* was printed by mistake in the June/July
number, p. 87.

C67. The Hawthorne Aspect [of Henry James]. *Little Review*, v. 4
(Aug. 1918) 47–53.

C68. A Note on Ezra Pound. *To-day*, iv. 19 (Sept. 1918) 3–9.

C69. 'Tarr'. *Egoist*, v. 8 (Sept. 1918) 105–6.
A review of *Tarr*, by Wyndham Lewis.

C70. FOUR POEMS. *Little Review*, v. 5 (Sept. 1918) 10–14.
*Contents*: Sweeney among the Nightingales—Whispers of
Immortality—Dans le Restaurant—Mr. Eliot's Sunday Morn-
ing Service.

C71. Studies in Contemporary Criticism. [i]. *Egoist*, v. 9 (Oct. 1918)
[113]–114.

C72. Studies in Contemporary Criticism. [ii]. *Egoist*, v. 10 (Nov./
Dec. 1918) 131–3.

C73. Marivaux. *Art and Letters*, ii. 2 (Spring 1919) 80–85.

C74. American Literature. *Athenaeum*, 4643 (Apr. 25, 1919) 236–7.
A review of *A History of American Literature*, *Vol. 2*, edited by
William P. Trent, John Erskine, Stuart P. Sherman, and Carl
Van Doren.

C75. A COOKING EGG. *Coterie*, 1 (May-day 1919) 44–45.

C76. A Romantic Patrician. *Athenaeum*, 4644 (May 2, 1919) 265–7.
A review of *Essays in Romantic Literature*, by George Wyndham; edited with an Introduction by Charles Whibley. Reprinted as 'A Romantic Aristocrat'.

C77. Kipling Redivivus. *Athenaeum*, 4645 (May 9, 1919) 297–8.
A review of *The Years Between*, by Rudyard Kipling.

C78. Kipling Redivivus. [A Letter] To the Editor. *Athenaeum*, 4646
(May 16, 1919) 344.

# C. *Contributions to Periodicals*

C79. A Sceptical Patrician. *Athenaeum*, 4647 (May 23, 1919) 361–2.
A review of *The Education of Henry Adams, An Autobiography*.

C80. Beyle and Balzac. *Athenaeum*, 4648 (May 30, 1919) 392–3.
A review of *A History of the French Novel, to the Close of the Nineteenth Century*, by George Saintsbury, vol. 2.

C81. Criticism in England. *Athenaeum*, 4650 (June 13, 1919) 456–7.
A review of *Old and New Masters*, by Robert Lynd.

C82. [TWO POEMS]. *Art and Letters*, II. 3 (Summer 1919) 103–5.
*Contents*: Burbank with a Baedeker: Bleistein with a Cigar—Sweeney Erect.

C83. The Education of Taste. *Athenaeum*, 4652 (June 27, 1919) 520–1.
A review of *English Literature during the Last Half-Century*, by J. W. Cunliffe.

C84. Reflections on Contemporary Poetry. [IV]. *Egoist*, VI. 3 (July 1919) 39–40.

C85. A Foreign Mind. *Athenaeum*, 4653 (July 4, 1919) 552–3.
A review of *The Cutting of an Agate*, by W. B. Yeats.

C86. The Romantic Generation, If It Existed. *Athenaeum*, 4655 (July 18, 1919) 616–17.
A review of *Currents and Eddies in the English Romantic Generation*, by Frederick E. Pierce.

C87. Whether Rostand had Something about Him. *Athenaeum*, 4656 (July 25, 1919) 665–6.
A review of *Le Vol de la Marseillaise*, by Edmond Rostand. Reprinted, with revision, as ' "Rhetoric" and Poetic Drama'.

C88. Was there a Scottish Literature? *Athenaeum*, 4657 (Aug. 1, 1919) 680–1.
A review of *Scottish Literature: Character and Influence*, by G. Gregory Smith.

C89. Some Notes on the Blank Verse of Christopher Marlowe. *Art & Letters*, II. 4 (Autumn 1919) 194–9.
Reprinted as 'Notes on the Blank Verse of Christopher Marlowe', and as 'Christopher Marlowe'.

C90. Tradition and the Individual Talent. [I]. *Egoist*, VI. 4 (Sept./Oct. 1919) 54–55.

C91. Swinburne and the Elizabethans. *Athenaeum*, 4664 (Sept. 19, 1919) 909–10.
A review of *Contemporaries of Shakespeare*, by A. C. Swinburne; edited by Edmund Gosse and T. J. Wise. Reprinted, with the addition of a paragraph at the end, as 'Swinburne as Critic'.

C92. Hamlet and His Problems. *Athenaeum*, 4665 (Sept. 26, 1919) 940–1.
A review of *The Problem of 'Hamlet'*, by the Right Hon. J. M. Robertson.

C93. Humanist, Artist, and Scientist. *Athenaeum*, 4667 (Oct. 10, 1919) 1014–15.

A review of *La Pensée Italienne au XVIme Siècle et le Courant Libertin*, by J. Roger Charbonnel, and *L'Éthique de Giordano Bruno et le Deuxième Dialogue du Spaccio, Traduction avec Notes et Commentaire*, by J. Roger Charbonnel.

C94. War-paint and Feathers. *Athenaeum*, 4668 (Oct. 17, 1919) 1036.

A review of *The Path on the Rainbow: An Anthology of Songs and Chants from the Indians of North America*, edited by George W. Cronyn.

C95. The Method of Mr. Pound. *Athenaeum*, 4669 (Oct. 24, 1919) 1065–6.

A review of *Quia Pauper Amavi*, by Ezra Pound.

C96. Our Inaccessible Heritage. [A Letter] To the Editor. *Athenaeum*, 4669 (Oct. 24, 1919) 1076.

C97. Tradition and the Individual Talent. [II]. *Egoist*, VI. 5 (Nov./Dec. 1919) 72–73.

C98. Mr. Pound and his Poetry. [A Letter] To the Editor. *Athenaeum*, 4671 (Nov. 7, 1919) 1163.

C99. Ben Jonson. *TLS*, 930 (Nov. 13, 1919) [637]–638.

C100. The Comedy of Humours. *Athenaeum*, 4672 (Nov. 14, 1919) 1180–1.

A review of *Ben Jonson*, by G. Gregory Smith, and *Ben Jonson's Every Man in his Humour*, edited by Percy Simpson.

C101. The Preacher as Artist. *Athenaeum*, 4674 (Nov. 28, 1919) 1252–3.

A review of *Donne's Sermons: Selected Passages*, with an Essay by Logan Pearsall Smith.

C102. The Local Flavour. *Athenaeum*, 4676 (Dec. 12, 1919) 1332–3.
A review of *Literary Studies*, by Charles Whibley.

C103. Swinburne. *Athenaeum*, 4681 (Jan. 16, 1920) 72–73.

A review of *Selections from Swinburne*, edited by Edmund Gosse and Thomas James Wise. Reprinted, with revision, as 'Swinburne as Poet'.

C104. 'The Duchess of Malfi' at the Lyric: and Poetic Drama. *Art & Letters*, III. 1 (Winter 1919/1920) 36–39.

C105. The Naked Man. *Athenaeum*, 4685 (Feb. 13, 1920) 208–9.
A review of *William Blake the Man*, by Charles Gardner. Reprinted as 'William Blake'.

C106. The Phoenix Society. [A Letter] To the Editor. *Athenaeum*, 4687 (Feb. 27, 1920) 285.

C107. A Brief Treatise on the Criticism of Poetry. *Chapbook*, II. 9 (Mar. 1920) 1–10.

# C. *Contributions to Periodicals*

This number of *The Chapbook* has a special title-page: Three Critical Essays on Modern English Poetry (By T. S. Eliot, Aldous Huxley, and F. S. Flint).

C108. Euripides and Gilbert Murray: A Performance at the Holborn Empire. *Art & Letters*, III. 2 (Spring 1920) 36–43.

C109. Dante as a 'Spiritual Leader'. *Athenaeum*, 4692 (Apr. 2, 1920) 441–2.
> A review of *Dante*, by Henry Dwight Sidgwick. Reprinted, with the addition of an introductory passage concerning Paul Valéry, as 'Dante'.

C110. The Poetic Drama. *Athenaeum*, 4698 (May 14, 1920) 635–6.
> A review of *Cinnamon and Angelica*, *A Play*, by John Middleton Murry.

C111. Philip Massinger. *TLS*, 958 (May 27, 1920) [325]–326.
> Reprinted as Part I of 'Philip Massinger'.

C112. The Old Comedy. *Athenaeum*, 4702 (June 11, 1920) 760–1.
> A review of *Philip Massinger*, by A. H. Cruickshank. Reprinted as Part II of 'Philip Massinger'.

C113. Artists and Men of Genius. [A Letter] To the Editor. *Athenaeum*, 4704 (June 25, 1920) 842.

C114. The Perfect Critic. [I]. *Athenaeum*, 4706 (July 9, 1920) 40–41.

C115. The Perfect Critic. II. *Athenaeum*, 4708 (July 23, 1920) 102–4.

C116. The Perfect Critic. [A Letter] To the Editor. *Athenaeum*, 4710 (Aug. 6, 1920) 190.

C117. The Possibility of a Poetic Drama. *Dial*, LXIX. 5 (Nov. 1920) [441]–447.
> Published simultaneously in *The Sacred Wood* (1920).

C118. The Second-Order Mind. *Dial*, LXIX. 6 (Dec. 1920) [586]–589.

C119. Andrew Marvell. *TLS*, 1002 (Mar. 31, 1921) [201]–202.

C120. London Letter. *Dial*, LXX. 4 (Apr. 1921) [448]–453.

C121. Prose and Verse. *Chapbook*, 22 (Apr. 1921) 3–10.
> This number of *The Chapbook* has a special title-page: Poetry in Prose, Three Essays by T. S. Eliot, Frederic Manning, Richard Aldington.

C122. London Letter. *Dial*, LXX. 6 (June 1921) [686]–691.

C123. John Dryden. *TLS*, 1012 (June 9, 1921) [361]–362.

C124. London Letter. *Dial*, LXXI. 2 (Aug. 1921) [213]–217.

C125. London Letter. *Dial*, LXXI. 4 (Oct. 1921) [452]–455.

C126. The Metaphysical Poets. *TLS*, 1031 (Oct. 20, 1921) [669]–670.

C127. Notes on Current Letters. *Tyro*, 1 (1922) [4].
> *Contents*: The Romantic Englishman, The Comic Spirit, and The Function of Criticism—The Lesson of Baudelaire.

## C. *Contributions to Periodicals*

C128. SONG TO THE OPHERIAN. *Tyro*, 1 (1922) 6.
    Signed with the pseudonym, Gus Krutzsch.

C129. The Three Provincialities. *Tyro*, 2 (1922) 11–13.
    Reprinted in *Essays in Criticism*, I. 1 (Jan. 1951) 38–41. See
    below No. 559.

C130. London Letter. *Dial*, LXXII. 5 (May 1922) [510]–513.

C131. Lettre d'Angleterre. [I]. *Nouvelle Revue Française*, IX. 104
    (May 1, 1922) 617–624.

C132. London Letter. *Dial*, LXXIII. 1 (July 1922) [94]–96.

C133. Answers to the Three Questions. *Chapbook*, 27 (July 1922) 8.

C134. London Letter. *Dial*, LXXIII. 3 (Sept. 1922) [329]–331.

C135. THE WASTE LAND. *Criterion*, I. 1 (Oct. 1922) 50–64.
    Without the 'Notes'. Reprinted in *The Dial*, LXXIII. 5
    (Nov. 1922) [473]–485.

C136. London Letter. *Dial*, LXXIII. 6 (Dec. 1922) [659]–662.
    Reprinted, with revision, as 'In Memoriam: Marie Lloyd' in
    *The Criterion*, I. 2 (Jan. 1923) 192–5, and as 'Marie Lloyd'.

C137. Lettre d'Angleterre [II]: Le Style dans la Prose Anglaise
    Contemporaine. *Nouvelle Revue Française*, X. 111 (Dec. 1,
    1922) 751–6.

C138. Dramatis Personæ. *Criterion*, I. 3 (Apr. 1923) 303–6.

C139. John Donne. *Nation & Athenaeum*, XXXIII. 10 (June 9, 1923)
    331–2.
    A review of *Love Poems of John Donne*. Nonesuch edition.

C140. Ben Jonson. [A Letter to the Editor]. *Nation & Athenaeum*,
    XXXIII. 13 (June 30, 1923) 426.

C141. The Function of a Literary Review. *Criterion*, I. 4 (July 1923)
    421.

C142. Contemporary English Prose. *Vanity Fair*, XX. 11 (July 1923)
    15.
    The revised English text of No. 137 above.

C143. Andrew Marvell. *Nation & Athenaeum*, XXXIII. 26 (Sept. 29,
    1923) 809.
    A review of *Miscellaneous Poems*, by Andrew Marvell.

C144. The Classics in France—and in England. *Criterion*, II. 5 (Oct.
    1923) 104–5.

C145. The Function of Criticism. *Criterion*, II. 5 (Oct. 1923) 31–42.

C146. The Beating of a Drum. *Nation and Athenaeum*, XXXIV. 1
    (Oct. 6, 1923) 11–12.
    A review of *Studies in the Development of the Fool in the
    Elizabethan Drama*, by Olive Mary Busby.

## C. Contributions to Periodicals

C147. Ulysses, Order, and Myth. *Dial*, LXXV. 5 (Nov. 1923) [480]–483.
A review of *Ulysses*, by James Joyce.

C148. A Preface to Modern Literature. *Vanity Fair*, XXI. 3 (Nov. 1923) 44, 118.
The revised English text of No. 131 above.

C149. Lettre d'Angleterre. [III]. *Nouvelle Revue Française*, XI. 122 (Nov. 1, 1923) 619–25.
Translated by G. D'Hangest.

C150. Marianne Moore. *Dial*, LXXV. 6 (Dec. 1923) [594]–597.
A review of *Poems* and *Marriage*.

C151. [A Letter to the Editor, F. M. Ford]. *Transatlantic Review*, I. 1 (Jan. 1924) 95–96.

C152. Four Elizabethan Dramatists. I. A Preface. *Criterion*, II. 6 (Feb. 1924) 115–23.

C153. A Prediction in Regard to Three English Authors, Writers who, though Masters of Thought, are likewise Masters of Art. *Vanity Fair*, XXI. 6 (Feb. 1924) 29, 98.
The authors concerned are Henry James, Sir James Frazer, and F. H. Bradley. The revised English text of No. 149 above.

C154. A Commentary. *Criterion*, II. 7 (Apr. 1924) 231–5. Signed: Crites.

C155. A Commentary. *Criterion*, II. 8 (July 1924) 371–5. Signed: Crites.

C156. [*A review of*] The Growth of Civilisation, and The Origin of Magic and Religion. By W. J. Perry. *Criterion*, II. 8 (July 1924) 489–91.

C157. A Commentary. *Criterion*, III. 9 (Oct. 1924) [1]–5. Signed: Crites.

C158. POÈME. *Commerce*, III (Winter 1924/1925) [9–11].
English text dated 'Nov. 1924', and French translation on opposite pages. English reprinted as Part I of 'The Hollow Men'.

C159. A Commentary. *Criterion*, III. 10 (Jan. 1925) 161–3. Signed: Crites.

C160. THREE POEMS. *Criterion*, III. 10 (Jan. 1925) 170–1.
*Contents*: I. Eyes I dare not meet in dreams—II. Eyes that last I saw in tears—III. The eyes are not here. The second of these poems is reprinted from *The Chapbook* (1924). The first and third were reprinted with changes as Parts II and IV of 'The Hollow Men'.

C161. On the Eve, A Dialogue. *Criterion*, III. 10 (Jan. 1925) 278–81.

## C. *Contributions to Periodicals*

C162. THE HOLLOW MEN, I–III. *Dial*, LXXVIII. 3 (Mar. 1925) [193]–194.

Reprinted as 'The Hollow Men', Parts I–II, and IV.

C163. A Commentary. *Criterion*, III. 11 (Apr. 1925) 341–4. Signed: Crites.

C164. The Ballet. *Criterion*, III. 11 (Apr. 1925) 441–3.

A review of *The Dance: An Historical Survey of Dancing in Europe*, by the late Cecil J. Sharpe . . . and A. P. Oppé, and *Mudras: The Ritual Hand Poses of the Buddha Priests and the Shiva Priests*, by Tyra de Kleen.

C165. Rencontre. *Nouvelle Revue Française*, XII. 139 (Apr. 1, 1925) [657]–658.

A tribute to Jacques Rivière.

C166. English Satire. *TLS*, 1247 (Dec. 10, 1925) 854.

A review of *English Satire and Satirists*, by Professor Hugh Walker.

C167. An Italian Critic on Donne and Crashaw. *TLS*, 1248 (Dec. 17, 1925) 878.

A review of *Secentismo e Marinismo in Inghilterra: John Donne—Richard Crashaw*, by Mario Praz.

C168. Shakespeare and Montaigne. *TLS*, 1249 (Dec. 24, 1925) 895.

A review of *Shakspere's Debt to Montaigne*, by George Coffin Taylor.

C169. Wanley and Chapman. *TLS*, 1250 (Dec. 31, 1925) 907.

A review of *Essays and Studies by Members of the English Association, Volume XI*; collected by Oliver Elton. There is some doubt as to Eliot's authorship of this review.

C170. The Idea of a Literary Review. *Criterion*, IV. 1 (Jan. 1926) 1–6.

C171. A Popular Shakespeare. *TLS*, 1255 (Feb. 4, 1926) 76.

A review of *The Works of Shakespeare, Chronologically Arranged*; with introductions by Charles Whibley, Volumes I–III.

C172. A Commentary. *Criterion*, IV. 2 (Apr. 1926) 221–3.

This and subsequent commentaries up to January, 1931, are unsigned, but were presumably written by T. S. Eliot and are consequently listed here.

C173. [*A review of*] All God's Chillun got Wings, Desire under the Elms, and Welded. By Eugene O'Neill. *Criterion*, IV. 2 (Apr. 1926) 395–6.

C174. Mr. Robertson and Mr. Shaw. *Criterion*, IV. 2 (Apr. 1926) 389–90.

A review of *Mr Shaw and 'The Maid'*, by the Rt. Hon. J. M. Robertson.

C175. A Commentary. *Criterion*, IV. 3 (June 1926) 417–20. Unsigned.

## C. *Contributions to Periodicals*

C176. English Verse Satire. *TLS*, 1273 (June 24, 1926) 429.
A review of *A Book of English Verse Satire*; chosen and annotated by A. G. Barnes.

C177. The Author of 'The Burning Babe'. *TLS*, 1278 (July 29, 1926) 508.
A review of *The Book of Robert Southwell*, by Christobel M. Hood.

C178. Plague Pamphlets. *TLS*, 1279 (Aug. 5, 1926) 522.
A review of *The Plague Pamphlets of Thomas Dekker*, edited by F. P. Wilson.

C179. Creative Criticism. *TLS*, 1280 (Aug. 12, 1926) 535.
A review of *Creative Criticism: Essays on the Unity of Genius and Taste*, by J. E. Spingarn.

C180. Chaucer's 'Troilus'. *TLS*, 1281 (Aug. 19, 1926) 547.
A review of *The Book of Troilus and Criseyde*, by Geoffrey Chaucer, edited by Robert Kilburn Root.

C181. American Prose. *TLS*, 1283 (Sept. 2, 1926) 577.
A review of *The Outlook for American Prose*, by Joseph Warren Beach; *S.P.E. Tract No XXIV: Notes on Relative Clauses*, by Otto Jespersen, and *American Slang*, by Fred Newton Scott. There is some doubt as to T. S. Eliot's authorship of this review.

C182. Lanceot Andrewes. *TLS*, 1286 (Sept. 23, 1926) [621]–622.

C183. A Commentary. *Criterion*, IV. 4 (Oct. 1926) 627–9. Unsigned.

C184. Mr. Read and M. Fernandez. *Criterion*, IV. 4 (Oct. 1926) 751–7.
A review of *Reason and Romanticism*, by Herbert Read, and *Messages*, by Ramon Fernandez.

C185. FRAGMENT OF A PROLOGUE. *Criterion*, IV. 4 (Oct. 1926) 713–18.
Pirated by Samuel Roth in his *Two Worlds Monthly*, II. 2 (Jan. 1927) 143–6.

C186. Hooker, Hobbes, and Others. *TLS*, 1293 (Nov. 11, 1926) 789.
A review of *The Social and Political Ideas of Some Great Thinkers of the Sixteenth and Seventeenth Centuries, A Series of Lectures*, edited by F. J. C. Hearnshaw.

C187. Massinger. *TLS*, 1294 (Nov. 18, 1926) 814.
A review of *Étude sur la Collaboration de Massinger avec Fletcher et Son Groupe*, par Maurice Chelli; and *Massinger's A New Way to Pay Old Debts*, edited by A. H. Cruickshank.

C188. More and Tudor Drama. *TLS*, 1296 (Dec. 2, 1926) 880.
A review of *Early Tudor Drama: Medwall, The Rastells, Heywood, and the More Circle*, by A. W. Reed.

C189. Medieval Philosophy. *TLS*, 1298 (Dec. 16, 1926) 929.

## C. *Contributions to Periodicals*

A review of *History of Mediæval Philosophy*, by Maurice de Wulf, Vol. 2: From St. Thomas Aquinas to the End of the Sixteenth Century.

C190. Mr. J. M. Robertson and Shakespeare. [A Letter to the Editor]. *Nation & Athenaeum*, XL. 11 (Dec. 18, 1926) 418.

C191. Whitman and Tennyson. *Nation & Athenaeum*, XL. 11 (Dec. 18, 1926) 426.

A review of *Whitman: An Interpretation in Narrative*, by Emory Holloway.

C192. A Commentary. *Criterion*, V. 1 (Jan. 1927) 1–6. Unsigned.

C193. FRAGMENT OF AN AGON. From *Wanna Go Home, Baby?* *Criterion*, IV. 1 (Jan. 1927) 74–80.

A pirated reprint appeared under title 'Wanna go home, baby? Fragment of an agon' in Samuel Roth's *Two Worlds Monthly*, III. 2 (May/June 1927) 149–52, the entire issue being dedicated to T. S. Eliot, also without his permission.

C194. Grammar and Usage. *Criterion*, V. 1 (Jan. 1927) 121–4.

A review of *Modern English Usage*, by H. W. Fowler; *The Philosophy of Grammar*, by Otto Jespersen; *A Grammar of Late Modern English*, by H. Poutsma; *Le Langage*, by J. Vendryes.

C195. Homage to Wilkie Collins. *Criterion*, V. 1 (Jan. 1927) 139–43.

A review of six mystery novels.

C196. A Note on Poetry and Belief. *Enemy*, 1 (Jan. [i.e. Feb.] 1927) 15–17.

C197. The Phoenix Nest. *TLS*, 1303 (Jan. 20, 1927) 41.

A review of *The Phoenix Nest*, reprinted from the original edition of 1593 (The Haslewood Books).

C198. Charleston, Hey! Hey! *Nation & Athenaeum*, XL. 17 (Jan. 29, 1927) 595.

A review of *The Future of Futurism*, by John Rodker; *Composition as Explanation*, by Gertrude Stein; *Pomona: or The Future of English*, by Basil de Selincourt; *Catchwords and Claptrap*, by Rose Macaulay.

C199. The Problems of the Shakespeare Sonnets. *Nation & Athenaeum*, XL. 19 (Feb. 12, 1927) 664, 666.

A review of *The Problems of the Shakespeare Sonnets*, by J. M. Robertson.

C200. Literature, Science, and Dogma. *Dial*, LXXXII. 3 (Mar. 1927) [239]–243.

A review of *Science and Property*, by I. A. Richards.

C201. A Study of Marlowe. *TLS*, 1309 (Mar. 3, 1927) 140.

A review of *Christopher Marlowe*, by U. M. Ellis-Fermor.

# C. *Contributions to Periodicals*

C202. Spinoza. *TLS*, 1316 (Apr. 21, 1927) 275.
A review of *The Oldest Biography of Spinoza*, edited by A. Wolf.

C203. 'Poet and Saint. . . .' *Dial*, LXXXII. 5 (May 1927) [424]–431.
A review of *Baudelaire: Prose and Poetry*; translated by Arthur Symons. Reprinted, with omission of first paragraph and other minor alterations, as 'Baudelaire in Our Time'.

C204. A Commentary. *Criterion*, v. 2 (May 1927) 187–90. Unsigned.

C205. Popular Theologians: Mr. Wells, Mr. Belloc and Mr. Murry. *Criterion*, v. 2 (May 1927) 253–9.
A review of *The Life of Jesus*, by J. Middleton Murry; *A Companion to Mr. Wells's Outline of History*, by Hilaire Belloc; *Mr Belloc Objects*, by H. G. Wells; *Mr Belloc Still Objects*, by Hilaire Belloc; *The Anglo-Catholic Faith*, by T. A. Lacey; *Modernism in the English Church*, by Percy Gardner.

C206. Le Roman Anglais Contemporain. *Nouvelle Revue Française*, XIV. 164 (May 1, 1927) [669]–675.

C207. Israfel. *Nation & Athenaeum*, XLI. 7 (May 21, 1927) 219.
A review of *Israfel: The Life and Times of Edgar Allan Poe*, by Hervey Allen; *Poems and Miscellanies of Edgar Allan Poe*, edited by R. Brimley Johnson; *Tales of Mystery*, by Edgar Allan Poe.

C208. A Commentary. *Criterion*, v. 3 (June 1927) 283–6. Unsigned.

C209. Recent Detective Fiction. *Criterion*, v. 3 (June 1927) 359–62.
A review of sixteen detective novels and of *Problems of Modern American Crime*, by Veronica and Paul King.

C210. Tennyson and Whitman. [A Letter to the Editor]. *Nation and Athenaeum*, XLI. 9 (June 4, 1927) 302.

C211. Nicolo Machiavelli (1469–1527.) *TLS*, 1324 (June 16, 1927) [413]–414.

C212. Thomas Middleton. *TLS*, 1326 (June 30, 1927) [445]–446.

C213. A Commentary. *Criterion*, IV. 1 (July 1927) 1–3. Unsigned.

C214. Political Theorists. *Criterion*, VI. 1 (July 1927) 69–73.
A review of *A Defence of Conservatism*, by Anthony M. Ludovici; *The Outline of Sanity*, by G. K. Chesterton; *The Servile State*, by Hilaire Belloc; *The Conditions of Industrial Peace*, by J. A. Hobson; *Coal*, by seven authors.

C215. Archbishop Bramhall. *Theology*, XV. 85 (July 1927) 11–17.
A review of *Archbishop Bramhall*, by W. J. Sparrow-Simpson. Reprinted as 'John Bramhall'.

C216. Plays of Ben Jonson. *TLS*, 1329 (July 21, 1927) 500.
A review of *Ben Jonson*, edited by C. H. Herford and Percy

Simpson, Volume III; *Eastward Hoe*, by Chapman, Jonson, and Marston, edited by Julia Hamlet Harris; *The Alchemist*, replica of first quarto.

C217. The Universities and the Daily Press. A Letter to the Editor. *British Weekly* (July 21, 1927).

C218. A Commentary. *Criterion*, VI. 2 (Aug. 1927) 97–100. Unsigned.

C219. Why Mr. Russell is a Christian. *Criterion*, VI. 2 (Aug. 1927) 177–9.
    A review of *Why I am not a Christian*, by the Hon. Bertrand Russell.

C220. Wilkie Collins and Dickens. *TLS*, 1331 (Aug. 4, 1927) [525]–526.

C221. The Twelfth Century. *TLS*, 1332 (Aug. 11, 1927) 542.
    A review of *The Renaissance of the Twelfth Century*, by Charles Homer Haskins.

C222. [*A review of*] The Playgoers' Handbook to the English Renaissance Drama, by Agnes Mure Mackenzie. *TLS*, 1334 (Aug. 25, 1927) 577.

C223. A Commentary. *Criterion*, VI. 3 (Sept. 1927) 193–6. Unsigned.

C224. [*A translation of*] Concerning 'Intuition', by Charles Mauron. *Criterion*, VI. 3 (Sept. 1927) 229–35.

C225. The Silurist. *Dial*, LXXXIII. 3 (Sept. 1927) [259]–263.
    A review of *On the Poems of Henry Vaughan: Characteristics and Intimations*, by Edmund Blunden.

C226. Crashaw's Poetical Works. *TLS*, 1337 (Sept. 15, 1927) 620.
    A review of *The Poems English, Latin and Greek of Richard Crashaw*; edited by L. C. Martin. There is some doubt as to T. S. Eliot's authorship of this review; it is not the same as No. 252.

C227. The Mysticism of Blake. *Nation & Athenaeum*, XLI. 24 (Sept. 17, 1927) 779.
    A review of six books by or about Blake.

C228. A Commentary. *Criterion*, VI. 4 (Oct. 1927) 289–91. Unsigned.

C229. Mr. Middleton Murry's Synthesis. *Criterion*, VI. 4 (Oct. 1927) 340–7.

C230. [*A translation of*] A Note on Intelligence and Intuition. By Ramon Fernandez. *Criterion*, VI. 4 (Oct. 1927) 332–9.

C231. Parnassus Biceps. *TLS*, 1342 (Oct. 20, 1927) 734.
    A review of *Parnassus Biceps; or, Several Choice Pieces of Poetry* (1656); edited by G. Thorn-Drury.

# C. *Contributions to Periodicals*

C232. Tristan da Cunha. [A Letter] To the Editor. *New Statesman,* xxx. 756 (Oct. 22, 1927) 44.
Concerns a poem by Roy Campbell.

C233. A Scholar's Essays. *TLS,* 1343 (Oct. 27, 1927) 757.
A review of *Nine Essays,* by Arthur Platt; with a preface by A. E. Housman.

C234. A Commentary. *Criterion,* vi. 5 (Nov. 1927) 385–8. Unsigned.

C235. [A Letter to] The Editor, 'The New York Evening Post', 26 July 1927 [with a further Letter, Aug. 22, 1927]. *Transition,* 9 (Dec. 1927) 185–6, 190.
Concerns Samuel Roth and his piracies (see above, No. 40, 185, 193).

C236. A Commentary. *Criterion,* vi. 6 (Dec. 1927) 481–3. Unsigned.

C237. Stage Studies. *TLS,* 1349 (Dec. 8, 1927) 927.
A review of *Pre-Restoration Stage Studies* and *The Physical Conditions of the Elizabethan Public Playhouse,* by William J. Lawrence.

C238. SALUTATION. *Saturday Review of Literature,* iv. 20 (Dec. 10, 1927) 429.
Reprinted in *The Criterion,* vii. 1 (Jan. 1928) 31–32, and as Part ii of *Ash-Wednesday.*

C239. Bradley's 'Ethical Studies'. *TLS,* 1352 (Dec. 29, 1927) [981]– 982.
Reprinted as 'Francis Herbert Bradley'.

C240. Mr. Chesterton (and Stevenson). *Nation & Athenaeum,* xlii. 3 (Dec. 31, 1927) 516.
A review of *Robert Louis Stevenson,* by G. K. Chesterton.

C241. A Commentary. *Criterion,* vii. 1 (Jan. 1928) 1–4. Unsigned.

C242. [*A translation of*] Prologue to An Essay on Criticism, by Charles Maurras. [i]. *Criterion,* vii (Jan. 1928) 5–15.

C243. Isolated Superiority. *Dial,* lxxxiv. 1 (Jan. 1928) [4]–7.
A review of *Personae: The Collected Poems of Ezra Pound.*

C244. An Emotional Unity. *Dial,* lxxxiv. 2 (Feb. 1928) [109]–112.
A review of *Selected Letters of Baron Friedrich von Hügel (1896–1924);* edited with a Memoir by Bernard Holland.

C245. A Commentary. *Criterion,* vii. 2 (Feb. 1928) 97–99. Unsigned.

C246. [*A translation of*] FROM 'ANABASE', by St. J. Perse. *Criterion,* vii. 2 (Feb. 1928) 137–8.

C247. Frenchified. [A Letter] To the Editor. *New Statesman,* xxx. 771 (Feb. 4, 1928) 528–9.

C248. The Criterion. [A Letter] To the Editor. *New Statesman,* xxx. 774 (Feb. 25, 1928) 622.

# C. *Contributions to Periodicals*

C249. A Commentary. *Criterion*, VII. 3 (Mar. 1928) 193–4. Unsigned.

C250. The *Action Française*, M. Maurras and Mr. Ward. *Criterion*, VII. 3 (Mar. 1928) 195–203.

C251. [*A translation of*] Prologue to an Essay on Criticism, by Charles Maurras. [II]. *Criterion*, VII. 3 (Mar. 1928) 204–18.

C252. The Poems English Latin and Greek of Richard Crashaw. *Dial*, LXXXIV. 3 (Mar. 1928) [246]–250.
A review of *The Poems English Latin and Greek of Richard Crashaw*; edited by L. C. Martin. Reprinted as 'A Note on Richard Crashaw'.

C253. PERCH' IO NON SPERO. *Commerce*, XV (Spring 1928) [5]–11.
English text and French translation on opposite pages. English reprinted as Part I of *Ash-Wednesday*.

C254. 'The Monthly Criterion' [A Letter to the Editor]. *Nation & Athenaeum*, XLIII. 3 (Apr. 21, 1928) 74.

C255. A Commentary. *Criterion*, VII. 4 (June 1928) 1–6. Unsigned.

C256. A Reply to Mr. Ward. *Criterion*, VII. 4 (June 1928) 84–88.

C257. Mr. Lucas's Webster. *Criterion*, VII. 4 (June 1928) 155–8.
A review of *The Complete Works of John Webster*; edited by F. L. Lucas.

C258. Parliament and the New Prayer Book. [A Letter] To the Editor. *New Adelphi*, I. 4 (June 1928) 345–6.

C259. The Idealism of Julien Benda. *Cambridge Review*, XLIX. 1218 (June 6, 1928) 485–8.
A review of *The Treason of the Intellectuals*, by Julien Benda. Reprinted in *The New Republic*, LVII. 732 (Pt. 2) (Dec. 12, 1928) 105–7.

C260. The Oxford Jonson. *Dial*, LXXXV. 1 (July 1928) [65]–68.
A review of *Ben Jonson*; edited by C. H. Herford and Percy Simpson, Volumes I, II, and III.

C261. The Humanism of Irving Babbitt. *Forum*, 80. 1 (July 1928) [37]–44.
Title given on wrapper is 'Can Humanism replace Religion?'

C262. Sir John Denham. *TLS*, 1379 (July 5, 1928) 501.
A review of *The Poetical Works of Sir John Denham*, edited by Theodore Howard Banks, Jr.

C263. An Extempore Exhumation. *Nation & Athenaeum*, XLIII. 14 (July 7, 1928) 470, 472.
A review of *The Skull of Swift*, by Shane Leslie.

C264. A Commentary. *Criterion*, VIII. 30 (Sept. 1928) 1–6. Unsigned.

C265. Civilisation: 1928 Model. *Criterion*, VIII. 30 (Sept. 1928) 161–4.
A review of *Civilization*, by Clive Bell.

# C. *Contributions to Periodicals*

C266. The Golden Ass of Apuleius. *Dial*, LXXXV. 3 (Sept. 1928) [254]–257.

A review of *The Golden Ass of Apuleius* . . . the Aldington translation . . . with an Essay by Charles Whibley.

C267. The New Censorship. [A Letter to the Editor]. *Nation & Athenaeum*, XLIII. 24 (Sept. 15, 1928) 755.

C268. Questions of Prose. [A Letter to the Editor]. *TLS*, 1391 (Sept. 27, 1928) 687.

C269. Three Reformers. *TLS*, 1397 (Nov. 8, 1928) 818.

A review of *Three Reformers: Luther, Descartes, Rousseau*, by Jacques Maritain.

C270. A Commentary. *Criterion*, VIII. 31 (Dec. 1928) 185–190. Unsigned.

C271. [*A translation of*] Fustel de Coulanges, by Pierre Gaxotte. *Criterion*, VIII. 31 (Dec. 1928) [258]–269.

C272. Freud's Illusions. *Criterion*, VIII. 31 (Dec. 1928) 350–3.

A review of *The Future of an Illusion*, by Sigmund Freud.

C273. Elizabeth and Essex. *TLS*, 1401 (Dec. 6, 1928) 959.

A review of *Elizabeth and Essex: A Tragic History*, by Lytton Strachey.

C274. The Literature of Fascism. *Criterion*, VIII. 31 (Dec. 1928) 280–90.

C275. American Critics. *TLS*, 1406 (Jan. 10, 1929) 24.

A review of *The Reinterpretation of American Literature*, edited by Norman Foerster.

C276. Introduction to Goethe. *Nation & Athenaeum*, XLIV. 15 (Jan. 12, 1929) 527.

A review of *Goethe and Faust: An Interpretation*, by F. Melian Stawell and G. Lowes Dickinson; *Goethe's Faust*, translated by Anna Swanwick.

C277. Turbervile's Ovid. *TLS*, 1407 (Jan. 17, 1929) 40.

A review of *The Heroycall Epistles of Ovid, translated into English Verse by George Turbervile*; edited with an introduction and glossary by Frederick Boas.

C278. Contemporary Literature. Is Modern Realism Frankness or Filth? [A Letter to the Editor.] *Forum*, LXXXI (Feb. 1929, Supplement) xlvi–xlvii.

C279. Mr. P. E. More's Essays. *TLS*, 1412 (Feb. 21, 1929) 136.

A review of *The Demon of the Absolute*, by Paul Elmer More.

C280. The Latin Tradition. *TLS*, 1415 (Mar. 14, 1929) 200.

A review of *Founders of the Middle Ages*, by Edward Kennard Rand.

# C. *Contributions to Periodicals*

C281. Sleeveless Errand [A Letter] To the Editor. *New Statesman,* XXXII. 830 (Mar. 23, 1929) 757.
Concerns the suppression of a book with this title by Norah James.

C282. A Commentary. *Criterion,* VIII. 32 (Apr. 1929) 377–81. Unsigned.

C283. Sherlock Holmes and His Times. *Criterion,* VIII. 32 (Apr. 1929) 552–6.
A review of *The Complete Sherlock Holmes Short Stories,* by Sir Arthur Conan Doyle; *The Leavenworth Case,* by Anna Katherine Green.

C284. A Letter [to the Editor]. *Little Review,* XII. 2 (May 1929) 90.

C285. Second Thoughts on Humanism. *New Adelphi,* II. 4 (June/Aug. 1929) [304]–310.
Reprinted as 'Second Thoughts about Humanism' in *Hound & Horn,* II. 4 (July/Sept. 1929) 339–50.

C286. The Tudor Translators. *Listener,* I. 22 (June 12, 1929) 833–4.

C287. The Elizabethan Grub Street. *Listener,* I. 23 (June 19, 1929) [853]–854.
'(From a talk on June 18).'

C288. The Genesis of Philosophic Prose: Bacon and Hooker. *Listener,* I. 24 (June 26, 1929) 907–8.
'(From a talk on June 25).' *At head of title*: Books and Authors.

C289. A Commentary. *Criterion,* VIII. 33 (July 1929) 575–9. Unsigned.

C290. Mr. Barnes and Mr. Rowse. *Criterion,* VIII. 33 (July 1929) 682–91.

C291. The Prose of the Preacher: The Sermons of Donne. *Listener,* II. 25 (July 3, 1929) 22–23.
'(From a talk on July 1).' *At head of title*: Books and Authors.

C292. Elizabethan Travellers' Tales. *Listener,* II. 26 (July 10, 1929) 59–60.
'(From a talk on July 9).' *At head of title*: Books and Authors.

C293. The Tudor Biographers. *Listener,* II. 27 (July 17, 1929) 94–95.
'(From a talk on July 16).'

C294. SOM DE L'ESCALINA. *Commerce,* XXI (Autumn 1929) [99]–103.
English text and French translation on opposite pages. English reprinted as Part III of *Ash-Wednesday.*

C295. A Commentary. *Criterion,* IX. 34 (Oct. 1929) 1–6. Unsigned.

C296. Experiment in Criticism. *Bookman,* LXX. 3 (Nov. 1929) 225–33.

# C. *Contributions to Periodicals*

C297. From a Distinguished Former St. Louisan. *St. Louis Globe Democrat* (1930).

John G. Neihardt's column 'Of Making Many Books' is devoted to a contribution entitled as above signed 'M. W. Childs' in which four paragraphs of a letter from Eliot to Childs concerning his memories of St. Louis are quoted. Part of this letter is reprinted by F. O. Matthiessen in the revised edition of *The Achievement of T. S. Eliot* (New York & London, Oxford University Press, 1947) p. 186.

C298. A Commentary. *Criterion*, IX. 35 (Jan. 1930) 181–4. Unsigned.

C299. [*A translation of*] A Humanist Theory of Value, by Ramon Fernandez. *Criterion*, IX. 35 (Jan. 1930) 228–45.

C300. [*A review of*] God: Being an Introduction to the Science of Metabiology. By J. Middleton Murry. *Criterion*, IX. 35 (Jan. 1930) 333–6.

C301. [*A review of*] Baudelaire and the Symbolists. Five Essays. By Peter Quennell. *Criterion*, IX. 35 (Jan. 1930) 357–9.

C302. Poetry and Propaganda. *Bookman*, LXX. 6 (Feb. 1930) 595–602.

C303. Thinking in Verse: A Survey of Early Seventeenth–Century Poetry. *Listener*, III. 61 (Mar. 12, 1930) 441–3.
'(From a talk on March 7)'.

C304. Rhyme and Reason: The Poetry of John Donne. *Listener*, III. 62 (Mar 19, 1930) 502–3.
'[From a talk on March 14 . . .].'

C305. The Devotional Poets of the Seventeenth Century: Donne, Herbert, Crashaw. *Listener*, III. 63 (Mar. 26, 1930) 552–3.
'(From a talk on March 21)'.

C306. A Commentary. *Criterion*, IX. 36 (Apr. 1930) 381–5. Unsigned.

C307. Mystic and Politician as Poet: Vaughan, Traherne, Marvell, Milton. *Listener*, III. 64 (Apr. 2, 1930) 590–1.
'(From a talk on March 28)'.

C308. The Minor Metaphysicals: From Cowley to Dryden. *Listener*, III. 65 (Apr. 9, 1930) 641–2.
'(From a talk on April 4)'.

C309. John Dryden. *Listener*, III. 66 (Apr. 16, 1930) 688–9.
'(From a talk on April 11)'. *At head of title*: Books and Authors.

C310. A Commentary. *Criterion*, IX. 37 (July 1930) 587–90. Unsigned.

C311. Arnold and Pater. *Bookman*, LXXII. 1 (Sept. 1930) 1–7.

C312. A Commentary. *Criterion*, IX. 38 (Oct. 1930) 1–4. Unsigned.

# C. *Contributions to Periodicals*

C313. [*A translation of*] On Reading Einstein, by Charles Mauron. *Criterion*, x. 38 (Oct. 1930) 23–31.

C314. Cyril Tourneur. *TLS*, 1502 (Nov. 13, 1930) [925]–926.

C315. A Commentary. *Criterion*, x. 39 (Jan. 1931) 307–14.
  This and all subsequent editorials are listed as 'By the Editor' and signed 'T.S.E.'.

C316. A Commentary. *Criterion*, x. 40 (Apr. 1931) 481–90.

C317. John Dryden—I. The Poet who Gave the English Speech. *Listener*, v. 118 (Apr. 15, 1931) 621–2.

C318. John Dryden—II. Dryden the Dramatist. *Listener*, v. 119 (Apr. 22, 1931) 681–2.

C319. John Dryden—III. Dryden the Critic, Defender of Sanity. *Listener*, v. 120 (Apr. 29, 1931) 724–5.

C320. [*A review of*] The Prospects of Humanism. By Lawrence Hyde. *English Review*, LIII. 1 (June 1931) 118, 120.

C321. A Commentary. *Criterion*, x. 41 (July 1931) 709–16.

C322. [*A review of*] Son of Woman: The Story of D. H. Lawrence. By John Middleton Murry. *Criterion*, x. 41 (July 1931) 768–74.

C323. [*A review of*] Essays of a Catholic Layman in England. By Hilaire Belloc. *English Review*, LIII. 2 (July 1931) 245–6.

C324. Thomas Heywood. *TLS*, 1539 (July 30, 1931) [589]–590.

C325. [*A review of*] Fashion in Literature: A Study of Changing Taste. By E. E. Kellett. *English Review*, LIII. 5 (Oct. 1931) 634–6.

C326. A Commentary. *Criterion*, XI. 42 (Oct. 1931) 65–72.

C327 DIFFICULTIES OF A STATESMAN. *Commerce*, XXIX (Winter 1931/1932) [79]–87.
  English text and French translation on opposite pages. English reprinted in *Hound & Horn*, VI. 1 (Oct./Dec. 1932) [17]–19.

C328. A Commentary. *Criterion*, XI. 43 (Jan. 1932) 268–75.

C329. George Herbert. *Spectator*, 5411 (Mar. 12, 1932) 360–1.

C330. Christianity and Communism. *Listener*, VII. 166 (Mar. 16, 1932) 382–3.
  *At head of title*: The Modern Dilemma.

C331. Religion and Science: A Phantom Dilemma. *Listener*, VII. 167 (Mar. 23, 1932) 428–9.
  *At head of title*: The Modern Dilemma.

C332. The Search for Moral Sanction. *Listener*, VII. 168 (Mar. 30, 1932) [445]–446, 480.
  *At head of title*: The Modern Dilemma.

# C. *Contributions to Periodicals*

C333. A Commentary. *Criterion*, XI. 44 (Apr. 1932) 467–73.

C334. Building up the Christian World. *Listener*, VII. 169 (Apr. 6, 1932) 501–2.
*At head of title*: The Modern Dilemma.

C335. John Ford. *TLS*, 1579 (May 5, 1932) [317]–318.

C336. A Commentary. *Criterion*, XI. 45 (July 1932) 676–83.

C337. A Commentary. *Criterion*, XII. 46 (Oct. 1932) 73–79.

C338. Apology for the Countess of Pembroke. *Harvard Graduates' Magazine*, XLI. 2 (Dec. 1932) 63–[75].

C339. FIVE-FINGER EXERCISES. *Criterion*, XII. 47 (Jan. 1933) 220–2.
*Contents*: I. Lines to a Persian Cat—II. Lines to a Yorkshire Terrier—III. Lines to a Duck in the Park—IV. For Ralph Hodgson Esqre.—V. For Cuscuscaraway and Mirza Murad Ali Beg.

C340. A Commentary. *Criterion*, XII. 47 (Jan. 1933) 244–9.

C341. English Poets as Letter Writers. *Yale Daily News*, LVI. 111 (Feb. 24, 1933) 3.
A review, with quotations, of the lecture which T. S. Eliot delivered on the Lamont Memorial Foundation in Sprague Hall, Yale University, on February 23, 1933. The lecture has not been published, but passages from it are quoted by Matthiessen in *The Achievement of T. S. Eliot*.

C342. A Commentary. *Criterion*, XII. 48 (Apr. 1933) 468–73.

C343. A Commentary. *Criterion*, XII. 49 (July 1933) 642–7.

C344. Address by T. S. Eliot, '06, to the Class of '33, June 17, 1933. *Milton Graduates Bulletin*, III. 9 (Nov. 1933) 5–9.
Taken down in shorthand without the speaker's knowledge and printed without correction.

C345. [*A review of*] Letters of Mrs. Gaskell and Charles Eliot Norton, 1855–1865. Edited with an Introduction by Jane Whitehill. *New England Quarterly*, VI. 3 (Sept. 1933) 627–8.

C346. Catholicism and International Order; Opening Address to the Anglo-Catholic Summer School of Sociology. *Christendom*, III. 11 (Sept. 1933) [171]–184.

C347. A Commentary. *Criterion*, XIII. 50 (Oct. 1933) 115–20.

C348. [*A review of*] The Name and Nature of Poetry. By A. E. Housman. *Criterion*, XIII. 50 (Oct. 1933) 151–4.

C349. The Modern Dilemma. *Christian Register*, CII. 41 (Oct. 19, 1933) [675]–676.
A modified reprint of an address made before a gathering of Unitarian clergymen in Boston.

# C. *Contributions to Periodicals*

C350. Personality and Demonic Possession. *Virginia Quarterly Review*, x. 1 (Jan. 1934) [94]–103.
    Reprinted, with alterations, as Part III of *After Strange Gods* (1934).

C351. A Commentary. *Criterion*, XIII. 51 (Jan. 1934) 270–8.

C352. Le Morte Darthur. *Spectator*, CLII. 5, 513 (Feb. 23, 1934) 278.
    A review of *Le Morte Darthur, reduced into Englisshe* by Sir Thomas Malory (The Shakespeare Head Press. 2 vols.).

C353. The Blackshirts. [A Letter to the Editor]. *Church Times*, CXI. 3, 706 (Feb. 2, 1934) 116.

C354. Tradition and Orthodoxy. *American Review*, II. 5 (Mar. 1934) 513–28.
    Reprinted, with alterations, as Part I of *After Strange Gods* (1934).

C355. Mr. Eliot's Virginian Lectures. [A Letter to the Editor]. *NEW*, IV. 22 (Mar. 15, 1934) 528.
    In reply to a review by Ezra Pound of *After Strange Gods*.

C356. The Theology of Economics. [A Letter to the Editor]. *NEW*, IV. 24 (Mar. 29, 1934) 575–6.

C357. A Commentary. *Criterion*, XIII. 52 (Apr. 1934) 451–4.

C358. WORDS FOR MUSIC: NEW HAMPSHIRE; VIRGINIA. *Virginia Quarterly Review*, x. 2 (Apr. 1934) [200].

C359. Mr. T. S. Eliot's Quandaries. [A Letter to the Editor]. *NEW*, IV. 26 (Apr. 12, 1934) 622–3.
    A further reply to Ezra Pound.

C360. Modern Heresies. [A Letter to the Editor] *NEW*, v. 3 (May 3, 1934) 71–72.

C361. 'The Use of Poetry' [A Letter to the Editor] *NEW*, v. 9 (June 14, 1934) 215.
    Another reply to Ezra Pound, signed: Possum.

C362. 'The Rock'. [A Letter] To the Editor. *Spectator*, 5528 (June 8, 1934) 887.

C363. [*A review of*] The Oxford Handbook of Religious Knowledge. *Criterion*, XIII. 53 (July 1934) 709.
    Signed, erroneously: T. McG.

C364. A Commentary. *Criterion*, XIII. 53 (July 1934) 624–30.

C365. [*A review of*] The Mystical Doctrine of St. John of the Cross. *Criterion*, XIII. 53 (July 1934) 709–10.
    Signed, erroneously: T. McG.

C366. [*A review of*] A Christian Sociology for To-day. (An abridged edition of 'Faith and Society'). By Maurice B. Reckitt. *Criterion*, XIII. 53 (July 1934) 710.

# C. *Contributions to Periodicals*

C367. John Marston. *TLS*, 1695 (July 26, 1934) [517]–518.

C368. The Problem of Education. *Harvard Advocate*, cxxi. 1 (Freshman Number 1934) 11–12.

C369. A Commentary. *Criterion*, xiv. 54 (Oct. 1934) 86–90.

C370. What does the Church stand for? *Spectator*, 5547 (Oct. 19, 1934) 560–1.

C371. Orage: Memories. *NEW*, vi. 5 (Nov. 15, 1934) 100.

C372. A Commentary. *Criterion*, xiv. 55 (Jan. 1935) 260–4.

C373. Notes on the Way [i]. *Time and Tide*, xvi. 1 (Jan. 5, 1935) 6–[7].

C374. Dowson's Poems. [A Letter] To the Editor. *TLS*, 1719 (Jan. 10, 1935) 21.

C375. Notes on the Way. [ii]. *Time and Tide*, xvi. 2 (Jan. 12, 1935) 33–34.

C376. Notes on the Way. [iii]. *Time and Tide*, xvi. 3 (Jan. 19, 1935) 88–90.

C377. T. S. Eliot's Notes on the Way. [A Letter to the Editor]. *Time and Tide*, xvi. 3 (Jan. 19, 1935) 95.

C378. Notes on the Way. [iv]. *Time and Tide*, xvi. 4 (Jan. 26, 1935) 118, 120–1.

C379. Mr Milne and War. [A Letter to the Editor]. *Time and Tide*, xvi. 4 (Jan. 26, 1935) 124.

C380. T. S. Eliot's 'Notes on the Way'. [A Letter to the Editor]. *Time and Tide*, xvi. 5 (Feb. 2, 1935) 154–5.

C381. Mr Milne and War. [A Letter to the Editor]. *Time and Tide*, xvi. 6 (Feb. 1935) 191.

C382. Douglas in the Church Assembly. [A Letter to the Editor]. *NEW*, vi. 18 (Feb. 14, 1935) 382–3.

C383. T. S. Eliot's 'Notes on the Way' [A Letter to the Editor]. *Time and Tide*, xvi. 8 (Feb. 23, 1935) 272.

C384. The Church Assembly and Social Credit. [A Letter to the Editor]. *NEW*, vi. 20 (Feb. 28, 1935) 422.

C385. The Church and Society. [A Letter to the Editor]. *NEW*, vi. 23 (Mar. 21, 1935) 482.

C386. A Commentary. *Criterion*, xiv. 56 (Apr. 1935) 431–6.

C387. Views and Reviews. [i]. *NEW*, vii. 8 (June 6, 1935) 151–2.

C388. Views and Reviews. [ii]. *NEW*, vii. 10 (June 20, 1935) 190–1.

C389. A Commentary. *Criterion*, xiv. 57 (July 1935) 610–13.
     Concerns W. B. Yeats.

C390. Views and Reviews. [iii]. *NEW*, vii. 18 (Sept. 12, 1935) 351–2.

# C. *Contributions to Periodicals*

C391. A Commentary. *Criterion*, xv. 58 (Oct. 1935) 65–69.

C392. Errata. [A Letter to the Editor]. *NEW*, vii. 22 (Oct. 10, 1935) 440.

C393. RANNOCH, BY GLENCOE. *NEW*, viii. 1 (Oct. 17, 1935) 10.
Reprinted in *New Democracy*, v. 8 (Dec. 15, 1935) 137.

C394. Pacifism. [A Letter to the Editor]. *NEW*, viii. 3 (Oct. 31, 1935) 58.

C395. Literature and the Modern World. *American Prefaces*, i. 2 (Nov. 1935) 19–22.
Reprinted in the same periodical, v. 9 (June 1940) 132–5.

C396. Views and Reviews. [iv]. *NEW*, viii. 4 (Nov. 7, 1935) 71–72.

C397. The Supernatural. [A Letter to the Editor]. *NEW*, viii. 5. (Nov. 14, 1935) 99.

C398. WORDS FOR AN OLD MAN. *NEW*, viii. 7 (Nov. 28, 1935) 131.
Reprinted as 'Lines for an Old Man'.

C399. Stilton Cheese. [A Letter] To the Editor. *Times*, London, 47,234 (Nov. 29, 1935) 15.

C400. Audiences, Producers, Plays, Poets. *New Verse*, 18 (Dec. 1935) 3–4.

C401. CAPE ANN. *New Democracy*, v. 8 (Dec. 15, 1935) 137.

C402. A Commentary. *Criterion*, xv. 59 (Jan. 1936) 265–9.

C403. [*A review of*] Totem: The Exploitation of Youth. By Harold Stovin. *Criterion*, xv. 59 (Jan. 1936) 363.
Unsigned, but ascribed to T. S. Eliot in the index.

C404. [*A review of*] Selected Shelburne Essays. By Paul Elmer More. *Criterion*, xv. 59 (Jan. 1936) 363.
Unsigned, but ascribed to T. S. Eliot in the index.

C405. The Church as Action: Note on a Recent Correspondence. *NEW*, viii. 23 (Mar. 19, 1936) 451.

C406. A Commentary. *Criterion*, xv. 60 (Apr. 1926) 458–63.

C407. The Church as Action. [A Letter to the Editor]. *NEW*, viii. 26 (Apr. 9, 1936) 523.

C408. The Church as Action. [A Letter to the Editor]. *NEW*, ix. 2 (Apr. 23, 1936) 38.

C409. A Commentary. *Criterion*, xv. 61 (July 1936) 663–8.

C410. The Year's Poetry. [A Letter to the Editor]. *Criterion*, xv. 61 (July 1936) 691.

C411. Mr Murry's Shakespeare. *Criterion*, xv. 61 (July 1936) 708–10.
A review of *Shakespeare*, by John Middleton Murry.

# C. *Contributions to Periodicals*

C412. Dr. Charles Harris. [A Letter to the Editor]. *Times*, London, 47,452 (Aug. 13, 1936) 12.

C413. A Commentary. *Criterion*, XVI. 62 (Oct. 1926) 63–69.

C414. The Need for Poetic Drama. *Listener*, XVI. 411 (Nov. 25, 1936) 994–5.
    Reprinted in *Good Speech*, VII. 35 (Apr./June 1937) 1–6.

C415. A Commentary. *Criterion*, XVI. 63 (Jan. 1937) 289–93.

C416. Paul Elmer More. *Princeton Alumni Weekly*, XXXVII. 17 (Feb. 5, 1937) [373]–374.

C417. The Church's Message to the World. *Listener*, XVII. 423 (Feb. 17, 1937) [293]–294, 326.
    Reprinted in *Christian Century*, LIV. 14 (Apr. 7, 1937) 450–2, and as an Appendix to *The Idea of a Christian Society* (1939).

C418. Mr. Reckitt, Mr. Tomlin, and The Crisis. *NEW*, x. 20 (Feb. 25, 1937) 391–3.

C419. A Commentary. *Criterion*, XVI. 64 (Apr. 1937) 469–74.

C420. Nightwood. *Criterion*, XVI. 64 (Apr. 1937) 560–4.
    A review of *Nightwood*, by Djuna Barnes; a reprint of the Introduction to the first American edition of the book.

C421. A Commentary. *Criterion*, XVI. 65 (July 1937) 666–70.

C422. The Church and the World. Problem of Common Social Action. *Times*, London, 47,739 (July 17, 1937) 18.
    A Report, with quotations, of T. S. Eliot's speech on 'The Ecumenical Nature of the Church . . .' delivered at Oxford on July 16.

C423. The Oxford Conference. [A Letter to the Editor]. *Church Times*, CXVIII. 3,889 (Aug. 6, 1937) 130.

C424. The Oxford Conference. [A Second Letter to the Editor]. *Church Times*, CXVIII, 3, 891 (Aug. 20, 1937) 184.

C425. Religious Drama: Mediæval and Modern. *University of Edinburgh Journal*, IX. 1 (Autumn 1937) 8–17.
    An Address delivered to the Friends of Rochester Cathedral.

C426. A Commentary. *Criterion*, XVII. 66 (Oct. 1937) 81–86.

C427. An Anglican Platonist: The Conversion of Elmer More. *TLS*, 1865 (Oct. 30, 1937) 792.
    A review of *Pages from an Oxford Diary*, by Paul Elmer More.

C428. *The Lion and The Fox* [of Wyndham Lewis]. *Twentieth Century Verse*, 6/7 (Nov./Dec. 1937) [6–9].

C429. A Commentary. *Criterion*, XVII. 67 (Jan. 1938) 254–9.

# C. *Contributions to Periodicals*

C430. Who Controls Population-Distribution? [A Letter to the Editor]. *NEW*, XII. 23 (Mar. 17, 1938) 459.

C431. Inquiry into the Spirit and Language of Night. [A Questionnaire answered by T. S. Eliot]. *Transition*, 27 (Apr./May 1938) 236.

C432. On a Recent Piece of Criticism. *Purpose*, x. 2 (Apr./June 1938) 90–94.
    Concerns 'The Mystery of Ezra Pound', by G. W. Stonier, published in *Purpose*.

C433. A Commentary. *Criterion*, XVII. 68 (Apr. 1938) 478–85.

C434. Mr T. S. Eliot on 'George Herbert'. *Salisbury and Winchester Journal* (May 27, 1938).
    A report, with quotations, of an Address to the Friends of Salisbury Cathedral given at the Chapter House, Salisbury, May 25, 1938.

C435. A Commentary. *Criterion*, XVII. 69 (July 1938) 686–92.

C436. Five points on Dramatic Writing. *Townsman*, I. 3 (July 1938) 10.
    'From a Letter to Ezra Pound. . . .'

C437. Professor H. H. Joachim. [A Letter to the Editor]. *Times*, London, 48,064 (Aug. 4, 1938) 12.

C438. A Commentary. *Criterion*, XVIII. 70 (Oct. 1938) 58–62.

C439. EIGHT POEMS. *Harvard Advocate*, CXXV. 3 (Dec. 1938) 9–16.
    A reprint of these contributions. Reprinted again in the same periodical, CXXXII. 2 (Nov. 1948) 3–7, with title 'The Undergraduate Poems of T. S. Eliot', and with the addition of 'Ode' ['For the hour that is left us Fair Harvard, with thee'].
    *Contents*: Song ['When we came home across the hill']—Song ['If space and time, as sages say']—Before Morning—Circe's Palace—On a Portrait—Nocturne—Humoresque [*sic*] After J. Laforgue—Spleen.

C440. Eliot on Bradley's Metaphysic. *Harvard Advocate*, CXXV. 3 (Dec. 1938) 24–26.
    T. S. Eliot's unpublished Harvard thesis, 'Experience and the Objects of Knowledge in the Philosophy of F. H. Bradley (1916)', is summarized and quoted from in this article by R. W. Church.

C441. [A Commentary] Last words. *Criterion*, XVIII. 71 (Jan. 1939) 269–75.

C442. Liberal Manifesto. [A Letter to the Editor]. *Church Times* (Jan. 27, 1939).

C443. A Commentary: That Poetry is made with Words. *NEW*, xv. 2 (Apr. 27, 1939) 27–28.

# C. *Contributions to Periodicals*

C444. 'That Poetry is made with Words.' [A Letter to the Editor]. *NEW*, xv. 4 (May 11, 1939) 66.

C445. A Commentary. On Reading Official Reports. *NEW*, xv. 4 (May 11, 1939) 61–62.

C446. The Idea of a Christian Society. *Purpose*, xi. 3 (July/Sept. 1939) 162–74.
  '. . . a chapter [i.e. Chapter i] from a book . . . to be published in the autumn.'

C447. Truth and Propaganda. [A Letter to the Editor]. *NEW*, xv. 22 (Sept. 14, 1939) 291.

C448. A Commentary [i]. *NEW*, xv. 25 (Oct. 5, 1939) 331–2.

C449. A sub-Pagan Society? *NEW*, xvi. 9 (Dec. 14, 1939) 125–6.

C450. Christian Society. [A Letter to the Editor]. *NEW*, xvi. 15 (Feb. 1, 1940) 226–7.

C451. Views and Reviews. Journalists of Yesterday and Today. *NEW*, xvi. 16 (Feb. 8, 1940) 237–8.

C452. Views and Reviews. On Going West. *NEW*, xvi. 17 (Feb. 15, 1940) 251.

C453. Education in a Christian Society. [A Letter to the Editor]. *Christian News-Letter*, Supplement No. 20 (Mar. 13, 1940) [1–4].

C454. EAST COKER. *NEW*, xvi. 22 (Mar. 21, 1940) [325]–328.
  An eighteen-line excerpt was reprinted in *Poetry*, lvi. 2 (May 1940) 109–10, and the entire poem in the *Partisan Review*, vii. 3 (May/June 1940) 181–7.

C455. Preface to the English Tradition. *Christendom*, x. 38 (June 1940) 101–8.

C456. Man and Society. *Spectator*, 5841 (June 7, 1940) 782.
  A review of *Man and Society in an Age of Reconstruction*, by Karl Mannheim.

C457. The Poetry of W. B. Yeats. *Purpose*, xii. 3/4 (July/Dec. 1940) 115–27.
  'The first Annual Yeats Lecture, delivered to the Friends of the Irish Academy at the Abbey Theatre, June, 1940.' Reprinted in *Southern Review*, vii. 3 (Winter 1941) 442–54.

C458. Hopousia. *Purpose*, xii. 3/4 (July/Dec. 1940) 154–8.
  A review of *Hopousia: or The Sexual and Economic Foundations of a New Society*, by J. D. Unwin. With an Introduction by Aldous Huxley.

C459. *Christian News-Letter*, Nos. 42, 43 (not including Supplement), 44 (Aug. 14, 21, 28, 1940).
  These three numbers were written by T. S. Eliot as guest-editor.

## C. *Contributions to Periodicals*

C460. The Writer as Artist: Discussion between T. S. Eliot and Desmond Hawkins. *Listener*, XXIV. 620 (Nov. 28, 1940) · 773–4.

C461. The English Tradition: Address to the School of Sociology. *Christendom*, X. 40 (Dec. 1940) [226]–237.

C462. A Commentary [II]. *NEW*, XVIII. 7 (Dec. 5, 1940) 75–76.

C463. Views and Reviews. Waiting at the Church. *NEW*, XVIII. 9 (Dec. 19, 1940) 99.

C464. The Malvern Conference. [A Letter] To the Editor. *Times*, London, 48,823 (Jan. 14, 1941) 5.
    Signed by Eliot, Hodges, and Vidler; dated January 12.

C465. THE DRY SALVAGES. *NEW*, XVIII. 19 (Feb. 27, 1941) [217–20].
    Reprinted in the *Partisan Review*, VIII. 3 (May/June 1941) 174–80.

C466. A Message to the Fish. *Horizon*, III. 15 (Mar. 1941) 173–5.
    Concerning the obituary notice of James Joyce in *The Times*, London (Jan. 14, 1941) p. 7.

C467. Towards a Christian Britain. *Listener*, XXV. 639 (Apr. 10, 1941) 524–5.

C468. Virginia Woolf. *Horizon*, III. 17 (May 1941) 313–16.

C469. Sir Hugh Walpole. [A Letter to the Editor]. *Times*, London, 48,945 (June 6, 1941) 7.

C470. Views and Reviews. Basic Revelation. *NEW*, XIX. 10 (June 26, 1941) 101–2.

C471. *Christian News-Letter*, No. 97 (Sept. 3, 1941).
    Written by T. S. Eliot as guest-editor.

C472. Greek Literature in Education. [A Letter to the Editor]. *NEW*, XX. 6 (Nov. 27, 1941) 52.

C473. Russian Ballet. [A Letter] To the Editor. *Times*, London, 49,105 (Dec. 10, 1941) 5.

C474. Greek Literature in Education. [A Letter to the Editor]. *NEW*, XX. 8 (Dec. 11, 1941) 72.

C475. 'The Duchess of Malfy'. *Listener*, XXVI. 675 (Dec. 18, 1941) 825–6.

C476. 'The Voice of His Time': T. S. Eliot on Tennyson's 'In Memoriam'. *Listener*, XXVII. 683 (Feb. 12, 1942) 211–12.

C477. A Letter to The Editors. *Partisan Review*, IX. 2 (Mar./Apr. 1942) 115–16.
    Concerns a lecture by Van Wyck Brooks on 'Primary Literature and Coterie Literature'; dated London, Jan. 5, 1942.

# C. *Contributions to Periodicals*

C478. In Praise of Kipling's Verse. *Harper's*, 185. 2 (July 1942) [149]–157.

> A condensed version of the Introduction to *A Choice of Kipling's Verse* (1941).

C479. *Christian News-Letter*, No. 141 (July 8, 1942).

> Written by T. S. Eliot as guest-editor.

C480. T. S. Eliot on Poetry in Wartime. *Common Sense*, XI. 10 (Oct. 1942) 351.

> Edited by T. S. Eliot from a radio address to a Swedish audience.

C481. LITTLE GIDDING. *NEW*, XXI. 26 (Oct. 15, 1942) 213–17.

C482. The Music of Poetry. *Partisan Review*, IX. 6 (Nov./Dec. 1942) 450–65.

> A reprint of *The Music of Poetry* (1942).

C483. Notes toward a Definition of Culture. I. *NEW*, XXII. 14 (Jan. 21, 1943) 117–18.

C484. Notes toward a Definition of Culture. II. *NEW*, XXII. 15 (Jan. 28, 1943) 129–30.

C485. Notes toward a Definition of Culture. III. *NEW*, XXII. 16 (Feb. 4, 1943) 136–7.

C486. Notes toward a Definition of Culture. IV. *NEW*, XXII. 17 (Feb. 11, 1943) 145–6.

> All four parts were reprinted in *Civilization*, XI (1944) 145–57, and in the *Partisan Review*, XI. 2 (Spring 1944) [145]–157. Published in revised form as 'Cultural Forces in the Human Order' in *Prospect for Christendom* ([1945]) and, further revised, as 'Chapter I. The Three Senses of Culture' in *Notes towards the Definition of Culture* ([1948]).

C487. 'A Dream within a Dream': T. S. Eliot on Edgar Allan Poe. *Listener*, XXIX. 737 (Feb. 25, 1943) 243–4.

C488. The Classics and the Man of Letters. *Groton School Quarterly*, XVI. 2 (Mar. 1943) [4]–13.

> A reprint of *The Classics and the Man of Letters* (1942).

C489. Education for Culture. [A Letter to the Editor]. *NEW*, XXII. 20 (Mar. 4, 1943) 176.

C490. South Indian Church. [A Letter] To the Editor. *Times*, London, 49,498 (Mar. 19, 1943) 5.

C491. South Indian Church. [A Letter] To the Editor. *Times*, London, 49,503 (Mar. 25, 1943) 5.

C492. John Dryden's Tragedies. *Listener*, XXIX. 745 (Apr. 22, 1943) 486–7.

C493. Planning and Religion. *Theology*, XLVI. 275 (May 1943) 102–6.

# C. *Contributions to Periodicals*

A review of *The Judgement of Nations*, by Mr. Christopher Dawson; *Diagnosis of Our Time*, by Dr. Karl Mannheim.

C494. The Approach to James Joyce. *Listener*, xxx. 770 (Oct. 14, 1943) 446–7.

C495. The Social Function of Poetry. *Norseman*, I. 6 (Nov. 1943) 449–57.
'. . . an extract from a lecture recently given at the British-Norwegian Institute in London.'

C496. Books across the Sea. [A Letter] To the Editor. *Times*, London, 49,698 (Nov. 9, 1943) 5.

C497. [A Letter in French to Ignace Legrand]. *Aguedal*, VII. 3/4 (Dec. 1943) 27.

C498. Responsibility and Power. *Christian News-Letter*, 196 (Dec. 1, 1943) Suppl. [1–4].

C499. T. S. Eliot on Kipling's Anti-Semitism. [A Letter to the Editor]. *Nation*, CLVIII. 3 (Jan. 15, 1944) 83.
Concerning L. Trilling's review of *A Choice of Kipling's Verse*.

C500. Aristocracy. [A Letter] To the Editor. *Times*, London, 49,832 (Apr. 17, 1944) 5.

C501. Books for the Freed World. [A Letter] To the Editor. *Times*, London, 49,850 (May 8, 1944) 5.

C502. The Responsibility of the Man of Letters in the Cultural Restoration of Europe. *Norseman*, II. 4 (July/Aug. 1944) 243–8.
Reprinted as 'The Man of Letters and the Future of Europe' in *Horizon*, x. 60 (Dec. 1944) [382]–389, and in the *Sewanee Review*, LIII. 3 (Summer 1945) [333]–342.

C503. Britain and America. Promotion of Mutual Understanding. *Times Educational Supplement*, 1540 (Nov. 4, 1944) 532.

C504. What is Minor Poetry? *Welsh Review*, III. 4 (Dec. 1944)[256]–267.
'The text of an Address delivered before the Association of Bookmen of Swansea and West Wales, at Swansea, September 26, 1944'. Reprinted in the *Sewanee Review*, LIV. 1 (Jan./Mar. 1946) 1–18.

C505. The 'Four Quartets'. [A Letter to the Editor]. *NEW*, xxvi. 15 (Jan. 25, 1945) 112.

C506. 'The Germanization of England'. [A Letter to the Editor]. *NEW*, xxvi. 21 (Mar. 8, 1945) 167–8.

C507. Full Employment and the Responsibility of Christians. *Christian News-Letter*, 230 (Mar. 21, 1945) 7–[12].
Signed with the pseudonym, Metoikos.

# C. *Contributions to Periodicals*

C508. 'The Germanisation of Britain'. [A Letter to the Editor]. *NEW*, xxvi. 24 (Mar. 29, 1945) 192.

C509. Cultural Diversity and European Unity. *Review*—45, ii. 2 (Summer 1945) 61–69.
'The text of an Address given . . . at the Czechoslovak Institute in April, 1945.'

C510. Mr. Charles Williams. *Times*, London, 50,144 (May 17, 1945) 7.
Obituary notice, written by T. S. Eliot, anonymously.

C511. The Social Function of Poetry. *Adelphi*, xxi. 4 (July/Sept. 1945) 152–61.
The original text of an Address delivered to an audience in Paris in May 1945; in part a modification of an Essay published originally in *Norseman*, i. 6 (Nov. 1943) 449–57 (No. 495 above).

C512. The Class and the Élite. *New English Review*, xi. 6 (Oct. 1945) 499–509.
Published in revised form as Chapter ii of *Notes towards the Definition of Culture* ([1948]).

C513. Mass Deportations. [A Letter] To the Editor. *Times*, London, 50,286 (Oct. 30, 1945) 5.

C514. Meaning of Culture. [A Letter to the Editor]. *Times Educational Supplement*, xxxvi. 1,593 (Nov. 10, 1945) 535.

C515. John Maynard Keynes. *NEW*, xxix. 5 (May 16, 1946) 47–48.
Written on the occasion of Lord Keynes's death.

C516. Reflections on the Unity of European Culture. [i]. *Adam*, xiv. 158 (May 1946) 1–3.

C517. Reflections on the Unity of European Culture (ii). *Adam*, xiv. 159/160 (June/July 1946) 1–3.

C518. Reflections on the Unity of European Culture (iii). *Adam*, xiv. 161 (Aug. 1946) 20–22.

C519. Ezra Pound. *Poetry*, lxviii. 6 (Sept. 1946) 326–38.
Reprinted in *NEW*, xxx. 3, 4 (Oct. 31, Nov. 7, 1946) 27–28, 37–39.

C520. 'Individualists in Verse'. [A Letter to the Editor]. *NEW*, xxx. 5 (Nov. 14, 1946) 52.
Signed: 'For Faber and Faber, Ltd., T. S. Eliot, Director'.

C521. The Significance of Charles Williams. *Listener*, xxxvi. 936 (Dec. 19, 1946) 894–5.

C522. Prufrock and Raskolnikov Again: A Letter from T. S. Eliot, by John C. Pope. *American Literature*, xviii. 4 (Jan. 1947) [319]–321.

# C. *Contributions to Periodicals*

Letter from T. S. Eliot to J. C. Pope, March 8, 1946, pp. [319]–320.

C523. 'Leçon de Valéry'. *Listener*, xxxvII. 939 (Jan. 9, 1947) 72.
The English text, reprinted from *Paul Valéry Vivant* (1946). Reprinted also in *Quarterly Review of Literature*, III. 3 (Spring 1947) [212]–214. The English text was recorded by T. S. Eliot and used by John Hayward in a B.B.C. broadcast Tribute to Valéry in Dec. 1947.

C524. 'Lord Bishops'. [A Letter] To the Editor. *Times*, London, 50,732 (Apr. 11, 1947) 5.

C525. UNESCO and the Philosopher. [A Letter] To the Editor. *Times*, London, 50,871 (Sept. 20, 1947) 5.

C526. UNESCO and Its Aims. The Definition of Culture. [A Letter] To the Editor. *Times*, London, 50,894 (Oct. 17, 1947) 7.

C527. UNESCO Policy. [A Letter] To the Editor. *Daily Mail* (London), Continental Edition, Paris (Nov. 12, 1947).

C528. On Milton [A Letter] To the Editor. *Sunday Times*, London (Nov. 16, 1947).

C529. UNESCO Policy. [A Letter] To the Editor. *Daily Mail* (London), Continental Edition, Paris (Dec. 26, 1947).

C530. 'Our Culture'. *NEW*, xxxII. 21 (Mar. 4, 1948) 203–4.
A review of *Our culture ... The Edward Alleyn Lectures*, 1944.

C531. Milton. *Sewanee Review*, LVI. 2 (Apr./June 1948) [185]–209.
A reprint of *Milton* (1947).

C532. Naturalized Subjects. [A Letter] To the Editor. *Times*, London, 51,065 (May 7, 1948) 5.

C533. Middleton Murry's 'The Free Society'. *Adelphi*, xxIV. 4 (July/ Sept. 1948) 245–7.
A review of *The Free Society*, by John Middleton Murry.

C534. A Personal Letter from T. S. Eliot. *Stage Door, the Magazine of the Newton Abbot Repertory Company*, I (Oct. 1948) 4–5.
Concerning a production of *Murder in the Cathedral*.

C535. TO WALTER DE LA MARE. *Tiger's Eye*, 6 (Dec. 1948) 16.
Reprinted from *Tribute to Walter de la Mare* ([1948]).

C536. Michael Roberts. *NEW*, xxxIV. 14 (Jan. 13, 1949) 164.
Reprinted in *The Marjohn* (magazine of the College of St. Mark and St. John, of which Roberts was Principal), Lent Term issue (1949).

C537. Leadership and Letters. *Milton Bulletin*, xII. 1 (Feb. 1949) [3]–16.
'War Memorial Address at Milton Academy, November 3, 1948.'

# C. *Contributions to Periodicals*

C538. The Report of the Lambeth Conference Criticized. *Guardian* (July 1, 1949).

C539. From Poe to Valéry. *Hudson Review*, II. 3 (Autumn 1949) [327]–342.
  A reprint of *From Poe to Valéry* (1948).

C540. Mr. Ezra Pound. [A Letter to the Editor]. *Scots Review* (Sept. 1949).

C541. A New Translation of the Bible [A Letter to the Editor]. *Theology*, LII. 351 (Sept. 1949).

C542. 'THE COCKTAIL PARTY'. *Life*, XXVII. 13 (Sept. 26, 1949) 16, 18, 20, 23.
  A Report of the première of the play at the Edinburgh International Festival, in which about sixty lines are quoted. The quotations were taken from an actor's typed copy and were the first appearance in print of any part of the play.

C543. A Message from T. S. Eliot, O.M. *Nine*, I. 1 (Oct. 1949) 6–7.
  A Letter addressed to Peter Russell, the Editor.

C544. The Aims of Poetic Drama. *Adam*, XVII. 200 (Nov. 1949) 10–16.
  '. . . part of a lecture . . . delivered before European audiences last month.' Published after extensive revision as *Poetry and Drama* (1951). This differs completely from the Address of the same title to the Poets' Theatre Guild, issued separately in London in 1949.

C545. Reflections on 'The Cocktail Party'. *World Review*, N.S. 9 (Nov. 1949) 19–22.
  T. S. Eliot's answers to fourteen questions about the play.

C546. T. S. Eliot on the Aims of Poetic Drama. *New York Herald Tribune*, CIX. 37,681 (Jan. 15, 1950) Section v, pp. 1, 2.
  A reprint, with minor omissions at beginning and end, of *The Aims of Poetic Drama* (1949).

C547. THE HUMAN MIND ANALYZED BY T. S. ELIOT. *New York Times Magazine* (Jan. 29, 1950) 14.
  About 145 lines of Sir Henry Harcourt-Reilly's speeches from *The Cocktail Party*

C548. Thanksgiving Fund. Relations with the University. [A Letter] To the Editor. *Times*, London, 51,662 (Apr. 11, 1950) 7.

C549. Students from Oversea. Scope of the Lord Mayor's Fund. [A Letter to the Editor]. *Times*, London, 51,667 (Apr. 17, 1950) 5.

C550. T. S. Eliot to Ezra Pound. *Hudson Review*, III. 1 (Spring 1950) 55–56.
  A letter, dated ⟨? January⟩ 1922, concerning *The Waste Land*. Reprinted in *Nine*, 4 (Summer 1950) 178–9.

## C. *Contributions to Periodicals*

C551. A Letter from T. S. Eliot. *Poetry*, LXXVI. 2 (May 1950) 88.

C552. Talk on Dante. *Italian News*, 2 (July 1950) 13–18.
A Lecture, 'What Dante means to me', delivered at the Italian Institute, London, on July 4, 1950. Reprinted in *The Adelphi*, XXVII. 2 (First Quarter 1951) 106–14.

C553. A Letter from T. S. Eliot, O.M. *Catacomb*, N.S. I. 1 (Summer 1950) 367–8.

C554. On Cultural Institutes. [A Letter] To the Editor. *Times*, London (July 11, 1950) 5.

C555. [A Letter to Jean Paulhan]. *Cahiers de la Pléiade*, X (Summer/ Autumn 1950) 27–29.
A Tribute to St. J. Perse, dated December 7, 1949. The French translation, by Dominique Aury, is titled 'Un Feuillet Unique' and is printed above the English text.

C556. POETRY BY T. S. ELIOT. An NBC Radio Discussion. *University of Chicago Round Table*, 659 (Nov. 12, 1950) 1–16.
A reading by T. S. Eliot of his poems, with Commentary.

C557. The Aims of Education. 1. Can 'Education' be Defined? *Measure*, II. 1 (Dec. 1950) [3]–16.
This, with Nos. 561, 562, and 564, below, constitutes the text of five Lectures delivered at the University of Chicago in Nov. 1950. A few copies of each were extracted from the magazine and stapled in the wrappers of the relevant issue.

C558. The Television Habit. [A Letter] To the Editor. *Times*, London (Dec. 20, 1950) 7.

C559. Postscript 1950 [to 'The Three Provincialities']. *Essays in Criticism*, I. 1 (Jan. 1951) 41.
The Essay itself is reprinted from *Tyro*, 2 (1922).

C560. Poetry and Drama. *Atlantic Monthly*, CLXXXVII. 2 (Feb. 1951) 30–37.
The first Theodore Spencer Memorial Lecture delivered at Harvard on November 21, 1950.

C561. The Aims of Education. 2. The Interrelation of Aims. *Measure*, II. 2 (Spring 1951) [191]–203.

C562. The Aims of Education. 3. The Conflict between Aims. *Measure*, II. 3 (Summer 1951) [285]–297.

C563. Norman Nicholson's 'Notes on the Way'. [A Letter to the Editor] *Time and Tide*, XXXII. 31 (Aug. 4, 1951) 746.

C564. The Aims of Education. 4. The Issue of Religion. *Measure*, II. 4 (Autumn 1951) [362]–375.

C565. The Value and Use of Cathedrals in England Today. *Friends of Chichester Cathedral Annual Report* (1950–51) 17–27.
An address given in Chichester Cathedral on June 16, 1951.

## C. *Contributions to Periodicals*

C566. Vergil and the Christian World. *Listener*, XLVI. 1176 (Sept. 14, 1951) 411–12, 423–4.

The text of the broadcast by the B.B.C. on Sept. 9, 1951.

C567. Those who need Privacy and Those whose Need is Company. *Cecil Houses ( Incorporated) 23rd Report* (1950–1) 15–17.

A report, with some omissions, from shorthand notes, of a speech in aid of Cecil Houses' Old Ladies Home, delivered at a Public Meeting in His Majesty's Theatre, London, on June 5, 1951.

C568. World Tribute to Bernard Shaw. [A Letter to the Editor]. *Time and Tide*, XXXII. 50 (Dec. 15, 1951) 1231–2.

# D

## TRANSLATIONS INTO FOREIGN LANGUAGES OF BOOKS, POEMS, AND ESSAYS BY T. S. ELIOT[1]

[1] *Arranged alphabetically by language and, within language groups, chronologically under the respective headings: 'Books', 'Anthologies', and 'Periodicals'. (Some foreign editions are listed in Section 3 of the Appendix.)*

*Titles of poems and volumes of poetry are printed in small capital letters.*

# D. *Translations into Foreign Languages*

## AFRIKAANS

D1. UIT'N VERTALING VAN 'EAST COKER'. *Groote Schuur*, Capetown, S.A. (1945) 27.
Two fragments, translated by N. G. Steytler.

## CHINESE

BOOK:

D2. [THE WASTE LAND, translated by Lo-jui Chen (Mme. Chen Meng-Chia), with an Introduction by Prof. K. C. Yeh. Shanghai, New Poetry Magazine, 193–?]. 146, [2] pp., incl. front.(port.) 17 × 12½ cm. Includes Bibliography of T. S. Eliot in English, pp. 123–43.

## CZECH

BOOKS:

D3. TAM DOMOV MÁŠ . . . Londýn, 1941. 1 blank leaf, 3 leaves, 9–22 pp., 1 leaf. 18½ × 13 cm. (Evergreen Series, 1). Title-page also in English. 750 copies, including 75 on Glastonbury Antique laid paper numbered and signed by T. S. Eliot and John Piper. A translation of *East Coker* by Libuše Pánková. On the third leaf is mounted a reproduction of a drawing by John Piper.

D4. NYNÍ A V ANGLII . . . Londýn, Faber a Faber [1944]. 23 pp. 23 cm. Title-page also in English. A translation, by Libuše Pánková, of *Little Gidding*.

D5. . . . PUSTÁ ZEMĚ. Praha, B. Stýblo, 1947. 1 blank leaf, 6 leaves, 15–56 pp., 3 leaves, 1 blank leaf, incl. 1 plate. 30½ × 21½ cm. 60 Kčs. A translation, by Jiřina Hauková and Jindřich Chalupecký, of *The Waste Land*.

PERIODICALS:

D6. KÁZÁNÍ OHNĚ. *Kvart*, 2 (Summer 1930) 90–94. A translation, by Arnošt Vaněček, of Part III of *The Waste Land*.

D7. HYSTERIE, *Kvart*, 2 (Summer 1930) 140. A translation, by Vaněček, of 'Hysteria'.

D8. TETA HELENA. *Kvart*, 2 (Summer 1930) 140. A translation, by Vaněček, of 'Aunt Helen'.

D*9. Tradice a Individuální Talent. *Listy pro Umění a Kritiku* (1934). A translation, by René Wellek, of 'Tradition and the Individual Talent'.

D10. PODOBIZNA DÁMY. *Listy*, I. 2 (June 15, 1946) [231]–234. A translation, by Jiřina Hauková, of 'Portrait of a Lady'.

D11. Hamlet. *Listy*, I. 4 (June 1, 1947) [535]–538. Translated by Jiři Mucha.


# DANISH

BOOKS:

D12. ... MORDET I DOMKIRKEN ... [København] Pauluskredsen, 1940. 62 pp., 1 blank leaf. 20 cm. 3.00. A translation, by N. J. Rald, of *Murder in the Cathedral*.

D13. ... Essays ... København, Steen Hasselbalchs Forlag, 1945. 63, [1] pp. 18½ cm. (Hasselbalchs Kultur-Bibliotek, Bind xlix). Translations, by Bjørn Poulsen, of 'Tradition and the Individual Talent', 'The Possibility of a Poetic Drama', 'Religion and Literature', and 'Baudelaire'.

D14. ... ØDEMARKEN OG ANDRE DIGTE ... København, Westermann, 1948. 86 pp., 1 leaf. 21½ cm. 885 copies, of which 235, issued in a slip-case, are on special paper and signed by author and translators. Translations, by Kai Friis Møller and Tom Kristensen, of 'Morning at the Window', 'Gerontion', 'The Hippopotamus', 'Sweeney among the Nightingales', *The Waste Land, Journey of the Magi*, and *Ash-Wednesday*.

D15. ... En Kristen Samfunds-Idé ... København, Wivels Forlag, 1948. 122 pp., 1 blank leaf, incl. plate(port.) 21 cm. 8.00. A translation, by Bjørn Poulsen, of *The Idea of a Christian Society*.

D16. FAMILIENS GENFORENING, ET SKUESPIL ... København, H. Hagerup, 1949. 1 blank leaf, 4 leaves, 11–129, [1] pp., 1 leaf. 21½ cm. 1,100 copies, of which 100, issued in a slip-case, are on special paper and signed by author and translator. A translation, by Kai Friis Møller, of *The Family Reunion*.

D17. ... COCKTAIL PARTY, EN KOMEDIE ... København, Steen Hasselbalchs Forlag, 1951. 170, [1] pp. 20½ cm. 10.00. Translated by Kai Friis Møller.


ANTHOLOGY:

D18. ENGELSKE DIGTE FRA VORE DAGE ved Kai Friis Møller. København, Det Berlingske Bogtrykkeri, 1943. 1 blank leaf, 3 leaves, 9–49 pp., 1 leaf, 2 blank leaves. 23 × 19 cm. 500 copies, plus 200 de luxe. Contains Møller's translations of 'Morning at the Window', and *Journey of the Magi*, pp. 39–41.

# D. *Translations into Foreign Languages*

# DUTCH

BOOKS:

D19. MOORD IN DE KATHEDRAAL . . . Brugge, Brussel, Amsterdam, De Kinkhoren, 1948. 1 blank leaf, 2 leaves, 7–88, [4] pp., 2 blank leaves. 4 plates. 20½ cm. 50.00 fr. (Opbouwen, 8. reeks, 59). A translation, by A. Frans Kern, of *Murder in the Cathedral*.

D20. BRAAKLAND, EEN GEDICHT. Amsterdam, G. A. Van Oorschot [1949]. 37 pp., 1 leaf. 21½ cm. 500 copies. A translation, by Theo van Baaren, of *The Waste Land*.

D21. . . . DE COCKTAILPARTY, EEN BLIJSPEL . . . Amsterdam, N. V. Em. Querido's Uitgeversmij, 1951. 156 pp., 2 leaves. 21 cm. Translated by M. Nijhoff.

ANTHOLOGY:

D22. Bert Voeten. DE AMMONSHOORN, GEDICHTEN. Amsterdam, De Bezige Bij [1949]. 66, [2] pp. 20 cm. Contains Voeten's translations of 'Morning at the Window', *Marina*, and *Journey of the Magi*, pp. 53–57.

PERIODICALS:

D*23. [THE WASTE LAND]. A Dutch translation of the poem was printed in the twenties 'in a "little magazine" of the vanguard kind, which lasted but a few issues'. I am indebted for this information to Mr. Angel Flores, but I have not been able to identify the periodical.

D24. Over de Eenheid der Europeesche Cultuur. *Internationale Echo*, II. 8 (Apr. 1947) [249]–256. An abridged translation of 'Reflections on the Unity of European Culture'.

D*25. TOCHT DER DRIE KONINGEN. *Vrij Nederland* (Oct. 2, 1948). A translation, by Bert Voeten, of *Journey of the Magi*.

D*26. EN TOT MIJN ZIEL ZEI IK. *Vrij Nederland* (Nov. 13, 1948). A translation (by St. John Blanchard Nixon?) of a 37-line excerpt from *East Coker*.

D27. OCHTEND AAN HET RAAM. *Kroniek van Kunst en Kultuur*, x. 1. (Jan. 1949) 47. A translation, by D. A. M. Binnendijk, of 'Morning at the Window'.

D28. DRIE GEDICHTEN. *Gids*, CXIII. 7 (July 1950) 1–7. Translations, by M. Nijhoff, of 'The Hippopotamus', 'The Love Song of J. Alfred Prufrock', and 'Lines for Cuscuscaraway and Mirza Murad Ali Beg'.

# D. *Translations into Foreign Languages*

## ESTHONIAN

PERIODICAL:

D29. LUULETISI. *Looming*, 5 (May 1929) 562–8. Translations, by
Ants Oras, of 'Preludes', 'Portrait of a Lady', 'The Hippopotamus', and 'The Hollow Men'.

## FINNISH

BOOKS:

D30. . . . AUTIO MAA, NELJÄ KVARTETTIA, JA MUITA RUNOJA. Helsinki,
Kustannusosakeyhtiö Otava [1949]. 183, [1] pp. 19½ cm. Os. 1.
Translations, by Yrjö Kaijärvi, Sinikka Kallio-Visapää, Kai
Laitinen, Juha Mannerkorpi, Kai Mäkinen, Leo Tiainen, and
Lauri Viljanen, of 'The Love Song of J. Alfred Prufrock',
'Morning at the Window', 'Aunt Helen', 'La Figlia che
Piange', 'Gerontion', 'Whispers of Immortality', *The Waste
Land*, 'The Hollow Men', *Ash-Wednesday, Journey of the Magi,
A Song for Simeon, Animula, Marina*, and *Four Quartets*.

D31. . . . COCKTAILKUTSUT, KOMEDIA. Helsingissä, Kustannusosakeyhtiö
Otava [1951]. 196 pp., 2 leaves. 19½ cm. Os. 1. Translated by
E. S. Repo and Ville Repo.

## FRENCH

BOOKS:

D32. . . . MEURTRE DANS LA CATHÉDRALE . . . Neuchâtel, Éditions de la
Baconnière [1943]. 3 leaves, 9–133, [1] pp., 4 leaves. 19½ cm.
(Cahiers du Rhône; Série Blanche). 4.50 fr. (Swiss). Also
twenty copies on vélin. A translation, by Henri Fluchère, of
*Murder in the Cathedral*. Reprinted, Neuchâtel, 1944, in the
same series, and published in Paris from 1946 by the Éditions
du Seuil in the series 'Pierres Vives'. Of the first impression of
this latter edition, there were fifty-five copies on vélin, five of
them not for sale.

D33. . . . Sommes-nous encore en Chrétienté? . . . Bruxelles, Éditions
Universitaires, Les Presses de Belgique [1946]. 1 blank leaf, 2
leaves, [vii]–xvii, 152 pp., 2 leaves, 1 blank leaf. 18½ cm.
(Collection 'Chrétienté Nouvelle' XII). A translation, by Albert
Frédérik, of *The Idea of a Christian Society*. Contains 'Préface
spéciale pour l'édition française', by T. S. Eliot, dated Novem-
ber 11, 1945: pp. [1]–6. This is translated by Frédérik, and the
English text has not been published.

# D. *Translations into Foreign Languages*

D34. . . . POÈMES 1910–1930 . . . Paris, Éditions du Seuil [1947]. 1 blank leaf, 3 leaves, 9–215 pp., 4 leaves. 17 × 13 cm. (Collection Poétique Bilingue). English and French on opposite pages. There were also 510 copies on vélin, ten of them not for sale. Translations, by Pierre Leyris, of 'The Love Song of J. Alfred Prufrock', 'Preludes', 'La Figlia che Piange', 'Morning at the Window', 'The Boston Evening Transcript', 'Aunt Helen', 'Mr. Apollinax', 'Gerontion', 'The Hippopotamus', 'Sweeney among the Nightingales', *The Waste Land* [with additional notes by John Hayward], *Ash-Wednesday, Journey of the Magi, A Song for Simeon, Animula,* and *Marina.* 'Lune de Miel' and 'Dans le Restaurant' are also included. Places and dates of composition are assigned to many of the poems.

D35. Rudyard Kipling: Poèmes, choisis et préfacés par T. S. Eliot . . . Paris, R. Laffont [1949]. 1 blank leaf, 2 leaves, [7]–473 pp., 1 leaf. 19½ cm. 800 fr. 3000 numbered copies. A translation, by Jules Castier, of *A Choice of Kipling's Verse.*

D36. . . . Essais Choisis . . . Paris, Éditions du Seuil [1950]. 1 blank leaf, 3 leaves, 9–410 pp., 3 leaves. 19 cm. (Collection 'Pierres Vives'). Also 105 copies on vélin, five of them not for sale. Translations, by Henri Fluchère, of twenty-one essays from *Selected Essays,* together with *What is a Classic?, Milton,* and the Aix Lecture 'Edgar Poe et la France', upon which *From Poe to Valéry* was based.

D37. . . . QUATRE QUATUORS . . . Paris, Éditions du Seuil [1950]. 1 blank leaf, 3 leaves, [9]–156 pp., 2 leaves. 17 × 13 cm. English and French on opposite pages. Also 205 copies on vélin, five of them not for sale. A translation, by Pierre Leyris, of *Four Quartets,* with notes by John Hayward.

ANTHOLOGIES:

D38. ANTHOLOGIE DE LA NOUVELLE POÉSIE AMÉRICAINE, par Eugène Jolas. Paris, Kra [1928]. 1 blank leaf, 3 leaves, 266 pp., 1 leaf. 19½ cm. 25 fr. Contains Jolas's translation of 'Portrait of a Lady', pp. [64]–69.

D39. Paul Valéry Vivant . . . [Marseille] Cahiers du Sud, 1946. 1 blank leaf, 2 leaves, [7]–381, [1] pp., 1 leaf. front.(port.), plates. 22½ cm. 320 fr. (For fuller description see above, B65.) Contains 'Leçon de Valéry', pp. [75]–81, as translated by Henri Fluchère.

D40. Maurice Le Breton. ANTHOLOGIE DE LA POÉSIE AMÉRICAINE CONTEMPORAINE. Paris, Les Éditions Denoël [1948]. 1 blank leaf, 3 leaves, 9–346 pp., 1 leaf. 19½ cm. 350 fr. Contains Le Breton's translation of 'The Love Song of J. Alfred Prufrock', pp. 254–63. English and French on opposite pages.

# D. *Translations into Foreign Languages*

D41. James Joyce, sa Vie, son Œuvre, son Rayonnement . . . Paris, La Hune, 1949. 63 leaves, 1 blank leaf, incl. plates, ports., facsims. 21 × 16½ cm. 400 fr. ($1.35). (For fuller description see above, B72.) Contains a translation of T. S. Eliot's prefatory note, verso of fifth leaf.

PERIODICALS:

D42. PRÉLUDES. *Écrits Nouveaux*, ix (Apr. 1922) [32]–33. Translations, by André Germain, of 'Preludes' and 'Morning at the Window'.

D43. POÈME. *Commerce*, III (Winter 1924/1925) [9–11]. A translation, by St.-J. Perse, of a poem later published as Part I of 'The Hollow Men'. English text, dated 'Nov. 1924', and French translation on opposite pages.

D44. LA CHANSON D'AMOUR DE J. ALFRED PRUFROCK. *Navire d'Argent*, 1 (June 1, 1925) [23]–29. A translation, by Sylvia Beach and Adrienne Monnier, of 'The Love Song of J. Alfred Prufrock'.

D45. LA TERRE MISE À NU. *Esprit*, 1 (May 1926) 174–94. A translation, by Jean de Menasce, of *The Waste Land*, carrying the note 'revue et approuvée par l'auteur'.

D46. Note sur Mallarmé et Poe. *Nouvelle Revue Française*, XIV. 158 (Nov. 1, 1926) [524]–526. Translated by Ramon Fernandez; English text not published.

D47. Deux Attitudes Mystiques: Dante et Donne. *Chroniques*, 3 (1927) 149–73. (Roseau d'Or, 14). A translation, by Jean de Menasce, of one of the unpublished Clark Lectures.

D48. PERCH' IO NON SPERO. *Commerce*, xv (Spring 1928) [5]–11. A translation, by Jean de Menasce, of a poem later published as Part I of *Ash-Wednesday*. English and French on opposite pages.

D49. CANTIQUE POUR SIMÉON. *Chroniques*, 7 (1929) 69–71. (Roseau d'Or, IV. 3). A translation, by Jean de Menasce, of *A Song for Simeon*.

D50. SOM DE L'ESCALINA. *Commerce*, XXI (Autumn 1929) [99]–103. A translation, by Jean de Menasce, of a poem later published as Part III of *Ash-Wednesday*. English and French on opposite pages.

D51. Courte Introduction à la Méthode de Paul Valéry. *Échanges*, 1 (Dec. 1929) [90]–94. A translation, by Georgette Camille, of 'A Brief Introduction to the Method of Paul Valéry'.

D52. DIFFICULTÉS D'UN HOMME D'ÉTAT. *Commerce*, XXIX (Winter 1931/1932) [79]–87. A translation, by Georges Limbour, of 'Difficulties of a Statesman'. English and French on opposite pages.

## D. *Translations into Foreign Languages*

D53. Les Caractères Féminins chez Thomas Middleton. *Cahiers du Sud*, No. spécial (June/July 1933) [204]–206. A translation, by Georgette Camille, of the latter half of 'Thomas Middleton'.

D54. MARINA. *Poésie*, XIII. 9 (Sept. 1934) 173–4. Translated by L. Bonnerot and A. Rivoallan.

D55. VOYAGE DES MAGES. *Mesures*, II. 3 (July 15, 1936) [53]–57. A translation, by Georges Cattaui, of *Journey of the Magi*. English and French on opposite pages.

D56. LES HOMMES CREUX. *Mesures*, II. 3 (July 15, 1936) [58]–67. A translation, by Georges Cattaui, of 'The Hollow Men'. English and French on opposite pages.

D57. Poésie Impersonnelle. *Messages*, I. 2 (1939) 51–[54]. A translation, by Geoffrey Stutfield and Jean Lescure, of Part II of 'Tradition and the Individual Talent'.

D58. MEURTRE DANS LA CATHÉDRALE (FRAGMENTS). *Cahiers du Sud*, XXVII (May 1940) [319]–328. A translation, by Henri Fluchère, of two choruses and some dialogue from *Murder in the Cathedral*. Certain fragments were also published in *Lettres* in 1942 or 1943 (see *Fontaine*, 30 (1943) 577).

D59. MERCREDI DES CENDRES. *Fontaine*, 27/28 (June/July 1943) 167–8. A translation, by Jean Wahl, of Part I of *Ash-Wednesday*.

D60. GERONTION. *Fontaine*, 27/28 (June/July 1943) 166–7. A translation, by Jean Wahl, of two passages from 'Gerontion'.

D61. LA FIGLIA CHE PIANGE. *Fontaine*, 27/28 (June/July 1943) 166. Translated by Jean Wahl.

D62. LES TROIS SAUVAGES. *Fontaine*, 27/28 (June/July 1943) [164]–165. A translation, by Yvan Goll, of Part I of *The Dry Salvages*.

D63. La Musique de la Poésie. *Fontaine*, 27/28 (June/July 1943) [17]–32. A translation, by Rachel Bespalof, of *The Music of Poetry*.

D64. LITTLE GIDDING. *Aguedal*, VII. 3/4 (Dec. 1943) 17–23. Translated by André Gide and Madeleine Bosco. Reprinted, in part, in *Choix*, I. 2 (1945) 32–34.

D65. Des Organes Publics et Privés de la Coopération Intellectuelle. *Fontaine*, 31 (1943) [1]–7.

D66. CANTIQUE DE SIMÉON. *Fontaine*, 37/40 (1944) [384]–385. A translation, by Sophie Deroisin, of *A Song for Simeon*. The English text is printed at the foot of the pages.

D67. BURNT NORTON. *Fontaine*, 37/40 (1944) 386–96. A translation, by Pierre Saffroy, carrying the note 'revue et approuvée par l'auteur'. The English text is printed at the foot of the pages.

D68. EAST COKER. *Lettres*, 2 (May 31, 1944) 24–[33]. Translated by Roger Montandon.

# D. *Translations into Foreign Languages*

D69. LITTLE GIDDING IV. *Formes et Couleurs*, VII. 2 (Mar. 1945) [73]. Translated by Jean Vogel.

D70. POÈMES. *Arts et Livres*, 3 (Apr. 1945) 3–5. Parts I and IV of *The Waste Land*, translated by Jean Bourrilly.

D71. L'Homme de Lettres et l'Avenir de l'Europe. *Table Ronde*, 2 (Apr. 1945) [89]–[104]. A translation, by Dominique Aury, of 'The Man of Letters and the Future of Europe'.

D72. Le Rôle Social du Poète. *Poésie 45*, VI. 25 (June/July 1945) 6–13. 'Fragments de la Conférence prononcée à Paris le 11 mai 1945.' Translated by Felix Rose. The English text was first printed as 'The Social Function of Poetry' in *The Adelphi*, July/September 1945.

D73. RAPSODIE POUR LE VENT DES TÉNÈBRES. *Saturne* (1946) 37–40. (Carte du Ciel, Cahiers de Poésie, 2). A translation, by Christian Dédéyan, of 'Rhapsody on a Windy Night'.

D74. TROIS POÈMES. *Fontaine*, 48/49 (Jan./Feb. 1946) [169]–188. Translations, by Pierre Leyris, of 'Preludes', 'Sweeney among the Nightingales', and 'The Fire Sermon' from *The Waste Land*. English text at foot of the pages.

D75. DEUX POÈMES D'ARIEL. *Clair de Terre* (1947) 137–41. (Carte du Ciel, Cahiers de Poésie, 3). Translations, by Pierre Leyris, of *Animula* and *Marina*.

D76. LA TERRE VAINE. *Licorne*, 1 (Spring 1947) [111]–137. A translation, by Pierre Leyris, of *The Waste Land*.

D77. GERONTION. *Poésie* 47, VIII. 38 (Mar. 1947) 2–7. Translated by Pierre Leyris. English and French on opposite pages.

D78. Réflexions sur l'Unité de la Culture Européenne. *Écho, Revue Internationale*, II. 8 (Apr. 1947) [247]–255. An abridged translation of 'Reflections on the Unity of European Culture'.

D79. [Hommage à Charles Maurras]. *Aspects de la France et du Monde*, II. 8 (Apr. 25, 1948) 6.

D80. Milton. *Table Ronde*, 6 (June 1948) [926]–955. Translated by Henri Fluchère.

D81. Les Poètes Metaphysiques. *Cahiers du Sud*, XXXV. 292 (1948) [487]–498. A translation, by Henry Fluchère, of 'The Metaphysical Poets'.

D82. EAST COKER. *Esprit et Vie* (Oct. 1948) [421]–428. Translated by Pierre Leyris.

D83. Baudelaire. *Revue Hommes et Mondes*, 29 (Dec. 1948) [541]–552. A translation of all save the last paragraph (Part IV) of T. S. Eliot's 'Introduction' to the *Intimate Journals*.

## D. *Translations into Foreign Languages*

D84. Edgar Poe et la France. *Table Ronde,* 12 (Dec. 1948) 1973–92. A translation, by Henri Fluchère, of the Lecture delivered at Aix in April, 1948, upon which *From Poe to Valéry* was based.

D85. LITTLE GIDDING. *Dieu Vivant,* 13 (1949) 69–81. Translated by Pierre Leyris.

D86. LA RÉUNION DE FAMILLE. *Âge Nouveau,* 49/50 (May 1950) 9–21. A translation, by Henri Fluchère, of Act III, Scene 2 of *The Family Reunion.*

D87. Un Feuillet Unique. *Cahiers de la Pléiade,* x (Summer/Autumn 1950) 27–29. A letter in homage to St.-J. Perse addressed to Jean Paulhan, the editor, and dated December 7, 1949. Translated by Dominique Aury, with the English text at the foot of the pages.

# GERMAN

BOOKS:

D88. MORD IM DOM . . . Berlin, Suhrkamp Verlag, 1946. 1 blank leaf, 4 leaves, 11–79, [1] pp. 20½ cm. A translation, by Rudolf Alexander Schröder, of the fourth English (1938) edition of *Murder in the Cathedral.* A new edition of this translation with title *Mord in der Kathedrale* was published in Vienna by Amandus-Edition in 1947.

D89. . . . Die Einheit der Europäischen Kultur. Berlin, Carl Habel Verlagsbuchhandlung, 1946. 63, [1] pp. 19 × 12½ cm. A translation, by Leonie Hiller, of 'The Unity of European Culture'. English and German on opposite pages. (For fuller description see above, A46).

D90. . . . VIER QUARTETTE . . . [Wien] Amandus-Edition, 1948. 39 pp. 22 cm. A translation, by Nora Wydenbruck, of *Four Quartets.*

D91. DER FAMILIENTAG, SCHAUSPIEL . . . Berlin, Suhrkampverlag, 1949. 120, [1] pp., 1 leaf. 20½ cm. DM 4.50. A translation, by Rudolf Alexander Schröder and Peter Suhrkamp, of *The Family Reunion.*

D92. . . . Die Idee einer Christlichen Gesellschaft. [Wien]Amandus-Verlag, 1949. 160 pp. 20 cm. A translation, by Herbert Furreg, of *The Idea of a Christian Society.*

D93. Beiträge zum Begriff der Kultur . . . [Berlin und Frankfurt-am-Main] Suhrkamp Verlag, 1949. 165, [1] pp., 1 leaf. 19 cm. DM 7. A translation, by Gerhard Hensel, of *Notes towards the Definition of Culture.*

D94. . . . Ausgewählte Essays 1917–1947. [Berlin und Frankfurt-am-Main] Suhrkamp Verlag, 1950. 513, [1] pp., 1 leaf. 19 cm. Selected by Hans Hennecke. Translations, by Ursula Clemen,

# D. *Translations into Foreign Languages*

Hans Hennecke, H. H. Schaeder, and W. E. Süskind, of selections chiefly from *The Use of Poetry and the Use of Criticism*; 'Tradition and the Individual Talent', 'The Function of Criticism', 'A Dialogue on Dramatic Poetry', 'Dante and Shakespeare [the Introduction to Knight's *Wheel of Fire*]', 'Hamlet', 'Ben Jonson', *Dante*, 'The Metaphysical Poets', *Milton*, 'William Blake', 'In Memoriam', 'Swinburne as Poet', 'Lancelot Andrewes', 'The *Pensées* of Pascal', 'Baudelaire', 'Marie Lloyd', 'The Humanism of Irving Babbitt', and *What is a Classic?*

D95. DIE COCKTAIL PARTY, EINE KOMÖDIE . . . Berlin und Frankfurt/Main, Suhrkamp Verlag, 1950. 169, [1] pp., 1 leaf. 20½ cm. Translated by Nora Wydenbruck. *On verso of title-page*: 1. bis 3. Auflage 1950.

D96. . . . AUSGEWÄHLTE GEDICHTE, ENGLISCH UND DEUTSCH. Frankfurt am Main, Suhrkamp Verlag, 1951. 149 pp., 1 leaf. 21½ cm. *On verso of title-page*: Erste bis dritte Auflage. Contains 'The Love Song of J. Alfred Prufrock', translated by Klaus Günther Just; *The Waste Land*, translated by Ernst Robert Curtius; *Ash-Wednesday*, translated by Rudolf Alexander Schröder, and *Four Quartets*, translated by Nora Wydenbruck. English and German on opposite pages.

D96a. James Joyce: Ausgewählte Prosa; ausgewählt und eingeleitet von T. S. Eliot; mit vollständiger Bibliographie und 4 Abbildungen. Zürich, Die Arche [1951]. 158 p., 1 leaf, incl. facsim. 2 plates (ports.) 19½ cm. (Sammlung Gestalten und Wege). A translation of *Introducing James Joyce* (1942), to which is added 'An Approach to James Joyce', translated as 'Ein biographisches Nachwort'. This and the Introduction are translated by Elisabeth Schnack; the selection from *Finnegans Wake*, by C. Gideon-Welcker, and the remainder of the text by Georg Goyert. Published also at Munich in 1951.

ANTHOLOGY:

D97. Hans Feist. EWIGES ENGLAND: DICHTUNG AUS SIEBEN JAHRHUNDERTEN VON CHAUCER BIS ELIOT. ENGLISH UND DEUTSCH. Zürich, Verlag Amstutz, Herdeg & Co. [1945]. 591, [1] pp. 24½ cm. Contains *Journey of the Magi, Animula, Marina, Ash-Wednesday* [I], *Burnt Norton* [V], Chorus from *The Rock*, and *The Dry Salvages* [IV], pp. 554–69. English and German on opposite pages.

PERIODICALS:

D98. DAS WÜSTE LAND. *Neue Schweizer Rundschau*, XX. 4 (Apr. 1, 1927) 362–77. A translation, by Ernst Robert Curtius, of *The Waste Land*. Reprinted in *Die Neue Rundschau*, LXI. 3 (1950) 327–45.

# D. *Translations into Foreign Languages*

D99. 'PERCH' IO NON SPERO'. *Neue Schweizer Rundschau* (Dec. 1930). A translation, by Max Rychner, of Part I of *Ash-Wednesday*.

D100. MORGEN AM FENSTER. *Silberboot*, 3 (June 1936) 105. A translation, by Hermann Broch, of 'Morning at the Window'.

D101. Tradition und individuelle Begabung. *Europäische Revue*, XII. 11 (Nov. 1936) 874–82. A translation, by Hans Hennecke, of 'Tradition and the Individual Talent'.

D102. Demokratie und Dichtung. *Innere Reich*, VI. 6 (Sept. 1938) 638–41. A translation, by Fritz Wölcken, of part of 'A Commentary', *Criterion*, XVII. 66 (Oct. 1937) 81–84.

D103. Pascal. *Neue Rundschau*, 1 (Jan. 1939) [25]–39. A translation of 'The *Pensées* of Pascal'.

D104. CHOR DER FRAUEN VON CANTERBURY. *Theater-Zeitung, Stadttheaters Basel*, XXIII. 18 (Jan. 15, 1939) 5–6. A translation, by Werner Wolff, of the Chorus beginning 'Here is no continuing city', printed in the programme for the performances of *Murder in the Cathedral* in Wolff's translation on January 20, 25, and 28, 1939.

D105. Eliot in seinen kritischen Schriften. *Schauspielhaus Zürich* [*Programme for performances of* The Family Reunion] (1944/1945) 6–8. Short passages, selected and translated by Fritz Meyer, from 'Tradition and the Individual Talent', *The Idea of a Christian Society*, and 'A Dialogue on Dramatic Poetry'.

D*106. EAST COKER. *Neue Schweizer Rundschau* (July 1945). A translation, by Hans Feist, of a fragment of the poem, beginning 'Dark, dark, dark . . .'.

D107. SOMMERMITTNACHT. *Neue Rundschau*, 1 (Oct. 1945) 108–9. A translation, by Richard Friedenthal, of Part I of *East Coker*.

D108. EAST COKER. *Wandlung*, I. 1 (Nov. 1945) [34]–45. Translated by Dolf Sternberger. English and German on opposite pages.

D109. Die gesellschaftliche Aufgabe der Dichtkunst. *Neue Auslese*, 7 (1946) 16–22. A translation of 'The Social Function of Poetry'.

D110. THE DRY SALVAGES. *Atlantis*, XVIII. 7 (July 1946) 319–24. Translated by Nora Wydenbruck. Preceded by the English text, pp. 317–19.

D111. CHOR DER FRAUEN VON CANTERBURY. *Schauspielhaus Zürich* [*Programme for performances of* Murder in the Cathedral] (1946/1947) 1–2. A translation, by R. A. Schröder, of the first Chorus from the play.

D112. Der Katholizismus und die Ordnung der Welt. *Turm*, II. 5/6 (1947) 178–81. A translation of 'Catholicism and the International Order'.

D113. Ein Telegramm von T. S. Eliot. *Turm*, II. 5/6 (1947) 227. Concerns the production of *Murder in the Cathedral* in Vienna.

# D. *Translations into Foreign Languages*

D114. REISE DER DREI KÖNIGE. *Wandlung*, II. 5 (June 1947) [425]–426. A translation, by Erich Kahler, of *The Journey of the Magi*. Preceded by the English text, p. [424].

D115. LA FIGLIA CHE PIANGE. *Göttinger Universitäts-Zeitung*, II. 23 (Nov. 7, 1947) 3.

D116. Was ist ein Klassiker? *Antike und Abendland*, III (1948) 9–25. A translation, by W. E. Süskind, of *What is a Classic?*

D117. Was ist ein Klassiker? *Merkur*, II. 1 (1948) 1–21. Another translation of *What is a Classic?*

D118. BURNT NORTON. *Deutsche Beiträge*, II. 6 (1948) 500–4. Translated by Ursula Clemen.

D119. MARINA. *Literarische Revue*, III. 9 (1948) 535. Translated by Franz Baermann Steiner.

D120. ASCHERMITTWOCH. *Göttinger Universitäts-Zeitung*, III (Feb. 13, 1948) 3. A free translation, by Dr. Dietrich Bischoff, of Part I of *Ash-Wednesday*. English and German in parallel columns.

D121. EAST COKER. *Neue Schweizer Rundschau*, XV. 12 (Apr. 1948) 743–8. Translated by Nora Wydenbruck.

D122. GEDICHTE. *Neue Rundschau*, 13 (Winter 1948/1949) [75]–84. Translations, by Kurt Heinrich Hansen, of a scene from *The Rock*; *Ash-Wednesday*, Part I; Song from *Sweeney Agonistes; A Song for Simeon*; and 'The Hollow Men'.

D123. Kulturelle Verschiedenheit und Europäische Einheit. *Thema*, 3 (1949) 11–13. Selections, translated by Fritz Volquard Arnold, from *Notes towards the Definition of Culture*.

D124. Über Kultur und Politik. *Neue Rundschau*, 14 (Spring 1949) [173]–185. A translation, by Gerhard Hensel, of Chapters III and IV of *Notes towards the Definition of Culture*.

D125. Die heutige Erziehung und die alten Sprachen. *Sammlung*, IV. 7 (July 1949) 397–404. A translation, by Dr. Helms, of 'Modern Education and the Classics'.

D126. PRÄLUDIEN. *Freie Presse*, Bielefeld, IV. 162 (Nov. 9, 1949) [8]. A translation of the first of the 'Preludes'.

D127. Die Aufgaben des Versdramas. *Neue Rundschau*, LXI. 2 (1950) [190]–203. A translation, by Friedrich Podszus, of 'The Aims of Poetic Drama'.

D128. DAS WÜSTE LAND. *Blätter der Städtischen Bühnen Düsseldorf* [*Programme for a performance of* The Family Reunion, *Feb. 10, 1950, p. 2*]. Part I, translated by K. H. Hansen.

D129. REISE DER DREI KÖNIGE. *Blätter der Städtischen Bühnen Düsseldorf* [*Programme, Feb. 10, 1950, p. 3*]. A translation, by Hansen, of *Journey of the Magi*.

## D. *Translations into Foreign Languages*

D130. Shakespeares Verskunst. *Monat*, II. 20 (May 1950) [198]–207. An unpublished lecture given on T. S. Eliot's German tour, and based upon earlier unpublished lectures on Shakespeare delivered in Edinburgh in 1937.

D130a. Zur Anabasis von Saint-John Perse. *Lot*, IV (Oct. 1950) [57]–59. A translation, by Leonharda Gescher, of T. S. Eliot's Introduction.

D131. Von Poe zu Valéry. *Merkur*, IV (Dec. 1950) 1252–67. A translation of *From Poe to Valéry*.

D132. Dichtung und Drama: Bemerkungen zur 'Cocktail Party'. *Universitas*, VI. 6 (June 1951) 645–8. A translation of parts of *Poetry and Drama*.


# GREEK

BOOK:

D133. [THE WASTE LAND AND OTHER POEMS. Athens, Ikaros, 1949]. 1 blank leaf, 3 leaves, 9–129 pp., 1 leaf. 27 cm. Translations, by George Seferis, originally published in Athens in 1936 in an edition of 120 copies, of *The Waste Land*, 'The Hollow Men', *Marina*, 'Difficulties of a Statesman', and Choruses from *Murder in the Cathedral*. A translation of 'Rhapsody on a Windy Night' is included in the notes.

D134. [MURDER IN THE CATHEDRAL. Athens, Damascos, 1949]. 1 blank leaf, 2 leaves, 7–120 pp., 1 leaf, 1 blank leaf. 21 cm. Translated by A. Zacharopoulos.


PERIODICALS:

D135. [POEMS]. *Kyklos*, II. 5 (July 1933) 185–213. Translations of 'Gerontion' and *The Waste Land* by T. K. Papatsones; *Ash-Wednesday* by N. Rantos; 'Dans le Restaurant' by M., and 'Lune de Miel' by Kaiser Emmanouel.

D136. THE DRY SALVAGES. *Tetradio Proto* (First Quarter 1945) 12–19. Translated by Alexander Xydes.

D137. [Reflections on the Unity of European Culture]. [*International Echo*] I. 1 (Mar. 1947) [1]–10. An abridged translation.

D138. [THE FAMILY REUNION, ACTS I–II]. *Aionas Mas*, 3–7 (May–Sept. 1949) 67–69, 101–4, 135–7, 175–7, 201–4. Translated by Zoe Karellis.

D*139. [A SONG FOR SIMEON]. *Prosperoe* (1949).

## D. *Translations into Foreign Languages*
## HEBREW

BOOK:

D140. [THE WASTE LAND. Tel-Aviv, Sefar, 1940]. 47, [1] pp. 19×11½ cm. Translated by Noah Stern.


## ITALIAN

BOOKS:

D*141. ASSASSINIO NELLA CATTEDRALE . . . Roma, tip. Failli, 1940. 16º, pp. xiv, 92. L. 3. (Teatro dell' Università di Roma. Collezione di Autori Stranieri, n. 1). An unauthorized translation, by Cesare Vico Lodovici, of the third English edition of *Murder in the Cathedral*; republished in Rome in 1943 and 1945 by Edizioni Italiane. (Title from *Bollettino delle Pubblicazioni Italiane* . . . 1940 (Firenze, 1941) No. 5483).

D142. . . . POESIE . . . Modena, Guanda Editore, 1941. 130 pp., 3 leaves. 19½×13 cm. (Collezione Fenice, 4). L. 12. Translations, by Luigi Berti, of 'The Love Song of J. Alfred Prufrock', 'Portrait of a Lady', 'Preludes', 'Rhapsody on a Windy Night', 'Morning at the Window', 'Gerontion', *The Waste Land*, 'The Hollow Men', *Journey of the Magi*, *Animula*, *Marina*, and *Ash-Wednesday*. This selection has been reprinted frequently since 1941, with additional poems in later editions.

D143. . . . Dante . . . Modena, Guanda Editore, 1942. 1 blank leaf, 3 leaves, 9–176 pp., 2 leaves. 19½ cm. (Collana di Cultura, 2). L. 15 (*raised to* 100). A translation, by Luigi Berti, of *Dante* (1929), 'Dante' (1920), and the Clark Lecture previously published only in French as 'Deux Attitudes Mystiques: Dante et Donne' (1927).

D144. LITTLE GIDDING . . . Edizioni Ali, 1944. 20 pp. 21½×15½ cm. (Poesia 1). L. 32. Translated by Raffaele La Capria and Tommaso Giglio.

D145. . . . Il Bosco Sacro: Saggi di Poesia e di Critica . . . Milano, Muggiani, 1946. 1 blank leaf, 5 leaves, 13–251 pp., 2 leaves. 22 cm. (Libri di Cultura, 3). L. 550. A translation, by L. Anceschi, of *The Sacred Wood*.

D146. Saggi Elisabettiani . . . [Milano, Firenze, Roma] Bompiani [1947]. 238, [2] pp. 21½ cm. (Portico: Critica e Saggi, 14). L. 320. A translation, by Alfredo Obertello, of *Elizabethan Essays*.

D147. ASSASSINIO NELLA CATTEDRALE . . . [Milano, Firenze, Roma] Bompiani [1947]. 89 pp., 1 leaf. 18 cm. (Pegaso Teatrale, 3). An authorized translation, by Alberto Castelli, of the fourth English edition of *Murder in the Cathedral*.

## D. *Translations into Foreign Languages*

D148. . . . L'Idea di una Società Cristiana . . . Milano, Edizioni di Comunità, 1948. 1 blank leaf, 2 leaves, 7-125 pp., 1 blank leaf. 23 cm. A translation, by Arigo Linder and Luciano Foà, of *The Idea of a Christian Society*. '. . . Nota Bibliographica', [4] pp. laid in at front.

D149. . . . LA TERRA DESOLATA, FRAMMENTO DI UN AGONE, MARCIA TRIONFALE. Firenze, Fussi [1949]. 1 blank leaf, 91 pp., 2 leaves, incl. 1 plate. 17 cm. L. 400. (Il Melagrano, 40–41). Translations, by Mario Praz, of *The Waste Land*, 'Fragment of an Agon', and *Triumphal March*. English and Italian on opposite pages. (For fuller description see above, No. B73).

D150. [An Italian translation of *The Cocktail Party* is in the press].

ANTHOLOGY:

D151. POETI AMERICANI (1662–1945), a cura di Gabriele Baldini. Torino, F. De Silva, 1949. 1 blank leaf, 3 leaves, ix–xxxiii, 434 pp., 1 leaf, 1 blank leaf. 10 plates(ports.) 21½ cm. (Maestri e Compagni, 15). L. 1600. Contains Baldini's translations of 'The Love Song of J. Alfred Prufrock', *The Waste Land*, 'The Wind sprang up at four o'clock', pp. 344–83. English and Italian on opposite pages.

PERIODICALS:

D152. LA TERRA DESOLATA. *Fiera Letteraria*, II. 8 (Feb. 21, 1926) 5. A translation, by Mario Praz, of Part v of *The Waste Land*.

D153. CANTO DI SIMEONE. *Solaria* (Dec. 1930). A translation, by Eugenio Montale, of *A Song for Simeon*. Reprinted in *Circoli*, III. 6 (Nov./Dec. 1933).

D154. [MARCIA TRIONFALE]. *Nuova Antologia*, CCCLX. 3 (Apr. 1, 1932) 428. A translation, by Mario Praz, of *Triumphal March*, printed in the course of his review of the English first edition.

D155. LA TERRA DESOLATA. *Circoli*, II. 4 (July/Aug. 1932) [27]–57. A translation, by Mario Praz, of *The Waste Land*.

D156. IL CANTO D'AMORE DI J. ALFRED PRUFROCK. *Letteratura*, I. 2 (Apr. 1937) [87]–90. A translation, by Luigi Berti, of 'The Love Song of J. Alfred Prufrock'.

D157. MERCOLEDÌ DELLE CENERI. *Letteratura*, I. 2 (Apr. 1937) [91]–96. A translation, by Luigi Berti, of *Ash-Wednesday*.

D158. FRAMMENTO DI UN AGONE. . . . *Letteratura*, I. 2 (Apr. 1937) [97]–102. A translation, by Mario Praz, of 'Fragment of an Agon'.

D159. EAST COKER. *Mese*, 5 (Feb. 1944) 60–62. A translation, by L. Montano, of Parts III and IV.

# D. *Translations into Foreign Languages*

D160. GLI UOMINI VUOTI. *Poesia*, Rome, I (Jan. 1945) 165–70. A translation, by Emilio Cecchi, of 'The Hollow Men'. English text printed at foot of the pages.

D161. EAST COKER. *Poesia*, I (Jan. 1945) 161–5. A translation, by Emilio Cecchi, of Parts I and v. English text at foot of pages.

D162. SOM DE L'ESCALINA. *Poesia*, I (Jan. 1945) 170–1. A translation, by Emilio Cecchi, of Part III of *Ash-Wednesday*. English text at foot of the pages.

D163. DAI CORI DELLA ROCCA. *Sud*, I. 3/4 (Jan. 15, 1946) 3. Part of a Chorus from *The Rock*, translated by R. La Capria.

D164. EAST COKER. *Sud*, I. 5/6 (Mar. 15, 1946) 7. Translated by T. Giglio and R. La Capria.

D165. Note per una Definizione della Cultura. *Inventario*, I. 1 (Spring 1946) [7]–18. A translation (by Luigi Berti?) of 'Notes towards the Definition of Culture'.

D166. L'Uomo di Lettere e l'Avvenire dell' Europa. *Inventario*, I. 3/4 (Autumn/Spring 1946/1947) [13]–18. A translation of 'The Man of Letters and the Future of Europe'.

D167. Un Poeta Americano Guida di Poeti Nuovi. *Fiera Letteraria*, II. 1 (Jan. 2, 1947) 3–4. A translation of 'Ezra Pound'.

D168. Che Cos' è un Classico? *Poesia*, Milan, VI (Mar. 1947) 11–31. A translation, by Jacopo Darca, of *What is a Classic?*

D169. TUTTO IL NOSTRO SAPERE. *Fiera Letteraria*, II. 25 (June 19, 1947). The first Chorus from *The Rock*, translated by Romeo Lucchese.

D170. Riflessioni sulla Unità della Cultura Europea. *Eco del Mondo*, II. 11 (July 1947) [633]–640. An abridged translation of 'Reflections on the Unity of European Culture'.

D171. MATTINO ALLA FINESTRA. *Adamo*, I. 2 (Oct. 20, 1947) [1]. A translation, by Virgilio Luciani, of 'Morning at the Window'.

D172. EAST COKER. *Tre Venezie*, XXI. 10/11/12 (Oct./Nov./Dec. 1947) 312–17. Translated by Margherita Guidacci.

D173. ANIMULA. *Immagine*, I. 5 (Nov./Dec. 1947) [296]–298. Translated by Eugenio Montale. English text at foot of pages. This number of the periodical is dedicated to T. S. Eliot.

D174. EAST COKER. *Immagine*, I. 5 (Nov./Dec. 1947) [299]–310. Translated by Emilio Cecchi. English text at foot of pages. See preceding entry.

D175. DA 'LA RIUNIONE DELLA FAMIGLIA'. *Fiera Letteraria*, III. 34 (Nov. 14, 1948) [1]. An extract, translated by Giorgio Melchiori, from Act II, Scene 2, of *The Family Reunion*. This number of the periodical is dedicated to T. S. Eliot.

## D. *Translations into Foreign Languages*

D176. Storia del Criterion. *Inventario*, II. 1 (Spring 1949) [1]–6. A translation of Part II of 'The Unity of European Culture'.

D177. Da Poe a Valéry. *Inventario*, III. 1 (Spring 1950) [40]–52. A translation, by Luigi Berti, of *From Poe to Valéry*.

D178. IL VIAGGIO DEI MAGI. *Pagine Nuove*, IV. 6/7 (June/July 1950) 277–8. A translation, by Virgilio Luciani, of *Journey of the Magi*.

D179. I Propositi del Dramma Poetico. *Inventario*, III. 2 (Summer 1950) [65]–[74]. A translation, by Luigi Berti, of part of 'The Aims of Poetic Drama'.

# JAPANESE

BOOKS:

D180. [Kan-zen naru hi-kyo ka . . . Tokyo, Kenkyusha, 1931]. 3 leaves, 55 pp., 1 leaf. 19½ cm. (Bun-gaku Ron Pamphlets). Translations, by Kitamura Tsuneo, of 'The Perfect Critic', and 'Tradition and the Individual Talent'.

D181. [Eliot Bun-gaku Ron . . . Tokyo, Kinseido, 1933]. 1 leaf, 389 pp., 1 leaf. 22½ cm. *Label on spine*: Selected Essays. Contains translations, by Kitamura Tsuneo, of 'Tradition and the Individual Talent', 'The Function of Criticism', 'A Brief Treatise on the Criticism of Poetry', 'The Metaphysical Poets', *Dante*, 'Hamlet', 'Swinburne as Critic', 'Arnold and Pater', 'Introduction' to Pound's *Selected Poems*, ' "Rhetoric" and Poetic Drama', 'The Humanism of Irving Babbitt', *John Dryden*, 'Baudelaire', 'Ben Jonson', 'Poetry and Propaganda', with an Introduction in English by William Empson, and a Bibliography in English.

D182. [Bun-gei hi-kyo-ron . . . Tokyo, Iwanami, 1940]. 125 pp., 2 leaves. 16 cm. Translations, by Yamoto Tadayoshi, of 'The Perfect Critic', 'Tradition and the Individual Talent', 'The Function of Criticism', 'Experiment in Criticism', 'The Metaphysical Poets', and 'Baudelaire'.

D183. [I-shin o ō-ité . . . Tokyo? Seikatsu-sha, 1943]. 1 leaf, 221 pp., 1 leaf. 18½ cm. Translations, by Nakabashi Kazuo, of *After Strange Gods*, 'Religion and Literature', 'Modern Education and the Classics', 'The *Pensées* of Pascal', and 'Niccolo Machiavelli'.

D184. [Shi no yō to hi-kyo-no yō . . . Tokyo? Zo-shin-sha, 1944]. 239 pp. 21½ cm. A translation, by Okamoto Masao, of *The Use of Poetry and the Use of Criticism*.

D185. [THE COCKTAIL PARTY; translated by Fukuda Tsune-ari. Tokyo, Koyama, 1951]. 300, [4] pp. front.(port.) 18½ cm. 250 yen.

## D. *Translations into Foreign Languages*

D186. [Notes towards the Definition of Culture; translated by Fukase Moto-hiro. Tokyo, Kō Bun Dō, 1951]. 2 leaves, 198 pp., incl. front.(port.) 18½ cm. 180 yen.

PERIODICAL:

D187. FOUR QUARTETS. *Shigaku* (Mar./Apr. 1951) 80–114. Translated by Kuri-yama Shū.

# NORWEGIAN

BOOKS:

D188. ... Fremmede Guder: En Elementarbok i Moderne Kjetteri ... Oslo, J. W. Cappelens Forlag [1948]. *55*, [1] pp. 20½ cm. (Cappelens Upopulære Skrifter). A translation, by Fredrik Wulfsberg, of *After Strange Gods*.

D189. ... DET GOLDE LANDET OG ANDRE DIKT ... Oslo, H. Aschehoug & Co., 1949. 83 pp. 22 cm. Translations, by Paal Brekke, of 'The Love Song of J. Alfred Prufrock', 'Gerontion', *The Waste Land*, 'The Hollow Men', *A Song for Simeon*, and *Ash-Wednesday*.

D190. ... Utvalgte Essays ... Oslo, E. G. Mortensens Forlag, 1950. 211 pp. 20½ cm. (Moderne Mestere). Translations, by Niels Chr. Brøgger, of 'Tradition and the Individual Talent', 'Religion and Literature', *The Idea of a Christian Society*, *What is a Classic?*, 'William Blake', 'The Humanism of Irving Babbitt', 'Second Thoughts about Humanism', 'The *Pensées* of Pascal', and 'Baudelaire'. Issued in paper and in boards.

D191. ... COCKTAIL-SELSKAPET, SKUESPILL I TRE AKTER ... Oslo, Gyldendal Norsk Forlag, 1951. 151 pp. 20 cm. (Gyldendals Moderne Skuespillserie). A translation, by Paal Brekke, of *The Cocktail Party*.

ANTHOLOGY:

D192. André Bjerke. FREMMEDE TONER: Et Utvalg av Verdenslyrikken i Norsk Gjendiktning. [Oslo] Dreyers Forlag, 1947. 9 leaves, 15–300 pp., 1 leaf, 1 blank leaf, incl. added t.-p., illus. in colour. 20½ cm. Contains Bjerke's translation of *Marina*, pp. 109–10.

PERIODICALS:

D193. MARINA. *Spektrum*, 4 (1947) 179–[180]. Translated by André Bjerke.

D194. 'Cocktail-selskapet' og Versdramaet. *Nationaltheatret, Oslo, Sesongen 1950–1951. Program* nr. 8, pp. 7, 9. An abridged translation (by Paal Brekke?) of *The Aims of Poetic Drama*.

# D. *Translations into Foreign Languages*
# PERSIAN

D*195. [THE WASTE LAND. 1938?]. 20 pp. 24 × 18½ cm. Translated by Aziz Ahmad. (The translator's presentation copy to T. S. Eliot is dated 'London, March 1938'.)

# POLISH

PERIODICALS:

D*196. [TRIUMPHAL MARCH]. *Pion*. Translated by Jósef Czechowicz.

D*197. [SONG FOR SIMEON; USK]. *Athenaeum*. Translated by Jósef Czechowicz. Mr. Czesław Milosz tells me that the above translations were published in Poland before the Second World War.

D198. . . . O Przetrwonie Naszej Cywilizacji. *Przegląd Polski*, I. 2 (Aug. 1946) 3–6. A translation, by Teresy Ichnowskiej, of the Introduction to *The Dark Side of the Moon*.

D199. WIERSZE. *Twórczość*, II. 10 (Oct. 1946) 5–22. Translations of *The Waste Land* by Czesław Milosz and 'The Hollow Men' by Władysław Dulęba.

# PORTUGUESE

PERIODICALS:

D200. A Função Social do Poeta. *Pensamento da América, Suplemento pan-Americano de A Manha*, Lisbon, v. 5 (June 2, 1946) [65]– 66, 68. A translation, by Pizarro Drummond, of 'The Social Function of Poetry'.

D201. A ROCHA. *Pensamento da América* (June 2, 1946) [65]. A Chorus from *The Rock*, translated by Pizarro Drummond.

D202. FRAGMENTO DO 'EAST COKER', *Jornal de Letras*, Rio de Janeiro (July 1949) 10. Part V, translated by Willy Lewin.

D203. POEMA DE ASH-WEDNESDAY. II. *Tavola Redonda. Folhas de Poesia*, 11 (Dec. 1951) [4–5]. A translation (facing the English text) by Fernando Guedes of *Ash-Wednesday*, II.

# RUMANIAN

BOOK:

D204. . . . CANTECUL DE IUBIRE AL LUI J. A. PRUFROCK . . . Cernăuți, Mircea Streinul, 1940. [7] pp. 29½ × 22½ cm. Lei 100. A translation, by Dragos Luta, of 'The Love Song of J. Alfred Prufrock'.

# D. *Translations into Foreign Languages*

## RUSSIAN

ANTHOLOGY:

D205. [M. Gutner. THE ANTHOLOGY OF NEW ENGLISH POETRY. Leningrad, 1937]. Contains Gutner's translations of 'Portrait of a Lady', 'The Hippopotamus' (two versions), *The Waste Land*, Part I, 'The Hollow Men', and a fragment from *The Rock*.

## SPANISH

BOOKS:

D206. TIERRA BALDÍA . . . Barcelona, Editorial Cervantes, 1930. 48 pp. 25 × 17½ cm. 3.50 ptas. A translation, by Angel Flores, of *The Waste Land*.

D207. . . . POEMAS . . . [Mexico City] Ediciones Taller, 1940. 1 blank leaf, 1 leaf, 5–47 pp., 1 leaf, 1 blank leaf. 24½ × 18 cm. 250 copies. Contains 'The Love Song of J. Alfred Prufrock', translated by Rodolfo Usigli; 'La Figlia che Piange', translated by Juan Ramón Jiménez; *The Waste Land*, translated by Angel Flores; 'The Hollow Men', translated by León Felipe; *Marina*, translated by J. R. Jiménez; *A Song for Simeon*, translated by Octavio G. Barreda; *Ash-Wednesday*, translated by B. Ortiz de Montellano; and 'Notes' to *The Waste Land*, translated by Angel Flores.

D208. La Idea de una Sociedad Cristiana . . . Buenos Aires, Mexico, Espasa-Calpe Argentina, s.a. [1942]. 1 blank leaf, 2 leaves, 7–158, pp., 1 blank leaf. 19 × 14½ cm. (Biblioteca Filosófica). $3 (m/arg). A translation, by Carlos M. Reyles, of *The Idea of a Christian Society*.

D209. . . . Los Poetas Metafísicos y Otros Ensayos sobre Teatro y Religión . . . Buenos Aires, Emecé Editores, S.A. [1944]. 2 v. 19 cm. (Colección Grandes Ensayistas, 7). $9.50 (m/arg). Also 55 numbered copies on special paper. A translation, by Sara Rubinstein, of *Selected Essays 1917–1932*.

D210. . . . POEMAS . . . Madrid, Editorial Hispanica, 1946. 1 blank leaf, 2 leaves, 7–83 pp., 5 leaves, 1 blank leaf. 15 × 11½ cm. (Adonais, XXVI). 6 ptas. 425 copies, plus 100 subscribers' copies on special paper. Contains 'Preludes', translated by Leopoldo Panero; 'La Figlia che Piange', translated by Dámaso Alonso; 'Portrait of a Lady', translated by José Luis Cano; *Ash-Wednesday*, translated by Charles David Ley; *Marina*, translated by L. Panero; *Journey of the Magi*, translated by D. Alonso; *A Song for Simeon* and 'Chorus IX' from *The Rock*, translated by José Luis Cano; and *East Coker*, translated by José A. Muñoz Rojas.

# D. *Translations into Foreign Languages*

D211. Henry James. Los Fantasmas del Castillo ('La Vuelta del Tornillo'). Traducción Autorizada del Original Inglés, por Juan Antonio Antequera; Prólogo de T. S. Elliot [*sic*]. Barcelona, 'Victoria' [1946]. 1 blank leaf, 2 leaves, 9–[199] pp., 1 blank leaf. 17 cm. 20 ptas. Contains 'Henry James y la Novella Inglesa Contemporánea, por T. S. Eliot': pp. 9–11, a translation of the first part of 'Le Roman Anglais Contemporain', an essay which appeared in *La Nouvelle Revue Française*, xiv. 164 (May 1, 1927) [669]–675.

D212. . . . MIÉRCOLES DE CENIZA: ASH WEDNESDAY. Mexico, Espiga, 1946. 1 blank leaf, 35 pp., 1 leaf. illus. 22 × 16 cm. A separate edition of the translation by B. Ortiz de Montellano included in D207 and originally printed in *Sur*, 48 (Sept. 1938) [20]–29.

D213. . . . Notas para la Definición de la Cultura. Buenos Aires, Emecé [1949]. 1 blank leaf, 4 leaves, 11–201 pp., 3 leaves. 19 cm. (Colección Grandes Ensayistas, 19). $8 (m/arg). A translation, by Jerónimo Alberto Arancibia, of *Notes towards the Definition of Culture*.

D214. . . . ASESINATO EN LA CATEDRAL. Madrid, 'Epesa', 1949. 2 blank leaves, 4 leaves, 13–136 pp., 3 leaves, 1 blank leaf. 1 illus. 'Prólogo del Autor para la Edición Española', pp. [25]–30. A translation, by Francisco de A. Carreres, of *Murder in the Cathedral*. The English text of T. S. Eliot's preface has not been published.

D215. . . . COCKTAIL PARTY. Buenos Aires, Emecé [1950]. 1 blank leaf, 3 leaves, 9–203, [1] pp., 3 leaves. 22 cm. (Teatro del Mundo). $16 (m/arg). Translated by Miguel Alfredo Olivera.

ANTHOLOGIES:

D216. Antología de Escritores Contemporáneos de los Estados Unidos; Prosa y Verso compilados por John Peale Bishop y Allen Tate; Versión de la Prosa a cargo de Ricardo A. Latcham; Versión de la Poesía a cargo de Varios Traductores . . . Santiago, Chile, Editorial Nascimento, 1944. 2 v. 21 cm. (*Date on spine*: 1945). Also on better paper, 23 cm. Vol. i contains Flores's translation of *The Waste Land*, Spanish and English on opposite pages, without the notes, pp. [366]–397; and a translation, by R. A. Latcham, of 'Tradition and the Individual Talent', pp. [538]–548.

D217. LA POESIA INGLESA. LOS CONTEMPORÁNEOS: Selección, Traducción y Prólogo de M. Manent. [Barcelona] Ediciones Lauro, 1948. 502 pp., 1 leaf. 20½ cm. English and Spanish on opposite pages. Contains translations of 'Morning at the Window', 'Aunt Helen', the first part of 'A Game of Chess', and 'Death by

# D. *Translations into Foreign Languages*

Water' from *The Waste Land*; *Journey of the Magi*, *A Song for Simeon*, two Choruses from *Murder in the Cathedral*, 'Landscapes', and *The Dry Salvages*, Part i, pp. 142–63.

D218. William Shand—Alberto Girri. POESÍA INGLESA CONTEMPORÁNEA. CONTEMPORARY ENGLISH POETRY. Prólogo de Patrick O. Dudgeon. Dibujos de Luis Seoane. [Buenos Aires] Editorial Nova [1948]. 1 blank leaf, 2 leaves, 7–98 pp., 1 leaf. $21\frac{1}{2} \times 16\frac{1}{2}$ cm. English and Spanish on opposite pages. Contains translations of 'La Figlia che Piange', *Journey of the Magi*, and 'The Hollow Men', pp. 42–53.

PERIODICALS:

D219. EL PARAMO. *Contemporáneos*, Mexico City, 26/27 (July/Aug. 1930) 15–32. A translation, by Enrique Munguià, Jr., of *The Waste Land*.

D220. LOS HOMBRES HUECOS. *Contemporáneos*, 33 (Feb. 1931) 132–6. A translation, by León Felipe, of 'The Hollow Men'.

D221. RAPSODÍA DE UNA NOCHE VENTOSA. *Sur*, Buenos Aires, 29 (Feb. 1937) [43]–46. A translation, by Julio Irazuzta, of 'Rhapsody of a Windy Night'.

D222. MIÉRCOLES DE CENIZA. *Sur*, 48 (Sept. 1938) [20]–29. A translation, by B. Ortiz de Montellano, of *Ash-Wednesday*.

D223. Poesía en Tiempos de Guerra. *Sur*, 99 (Dec. 1942) [27]–29. A translation of 'T. S. Eliot on Poetry in Wartime'.

D224. La Música de la Poesía. *Atenea*, Santiago, Chile, LXXIII. 219 (Sept. 1943) [251]–274. A translation, by Octavio G. Barreda, of *The Music of Poetry*.

D225. Notas para una Definición de la Cultura. *Asomante*, San Juan, Puerto Rico, I. 3 (July/Sept. 1945) 7–22. A translation, by Ramón Lavandero, of 'Notes toward a Definition of Culture'.

D226. EAST COKER. *Orígenes*, La Habana, Cuba, III. 9 (Spring 1946) 21–27. Translated by José Rodríguez Feo.

D227. ¿Qué es un Clásico? *Sur*, 153/156 (July/Oct. 1947) [18]–44. A translation, by E. L. Revol, of *What is a Classic?*

D228. LITTLE GIDDING (FRAGMENTO). *Sur*, 153/156 (July/Oct. 1947) [366]–369. A translation, by E. L. Revol, of the first section of Part v. English and Spanish on opposite pages.

D229. Ezra Pound. *Moradas*, Lima, Peru, I. 3 (Dec. 1947/Jan. 1948) [233]–241. Translated by Raúl Deustua.

D230. Milton. *Realidad*, Buenos Aires, II. 4 (July/Aug. 1948) [1]–27.

D231. MIÉRCOLES DE CENIZA. *Pro Arte*, Santiago, Chile, I. 6 (Aug. 19, 1948). A translation, by Jorge Elliott García, of *Ash-Wednesday*.

# D. *Translations into Foreign Languages*

D232. COROS DE 'CRIMEN EN LA CATEDRAL'. *Pro Arte*, I. 18 (Nov. 11, 1948) 1, 6.

D233. AUTORRETRATO BURLESCO. *Pro Arte*, I. 18 (Nov. 11, 1948) 1. A free translation, by Santiago del Campo, of 'For Cuscuscaraway and Mirza Murad Ali Beg'. English text precedes the Spanish.

D234. [Selections]. *Hora*, Madrid (Dec. 1948). Translations of parts of *Burnt Norton*, 'Difficulties of a Statesman', and 'Hamlet'.

D235. CRIMEN EN LA CATEDRAL [I–III]. *Número*, Montevideo, I. 1–3 (Mar./Apr.-July/Aug. 1949) [?], 123–39, [201]–220. A translation, by I. Vilariño and E. Rodríguez Monegal, of *Murder in the Cathedral*.

D236. LOS TRES SALVAJES. *Armas y Letras*, Bogotá, Colombia, II. 4 (June 1949) [3]–8. A translation, by Jaime Tello, of *The Dry Salvages*.

D237. CUATRO CUARTETOS. *Escritura*, Montevideo, Uruguay, III. 7 (June 1949) [5]–34. A translation, with notes (pp. 35–39), by Américo Barabino, of *Four Quartets*.

# SWEDISH

BOOKS:

D238. MORDET I KATEDRALEN . . . Stockholm, Albert Bonniers Förlag [1939]. 97 pp., 1 blank leaf. 19½ cm. (Sv. Teatern, 441). 3 kr. A translation, by Erik Lindegren and Karl Vennberg, of *Murder in the Cathedral*.

D239. . . . DIKTER . . . Stockholm, Albert Bonniers Förlag [1942]. xliii, 86, [1] pp., 1 leaf. 20 cm. 5.75 kr. Contains 'The Love Song of J. Alfred Prufrock', translated by Gunnar Ekelöf; 'Morning at the Window', and 'La Figlia che Piange', translated by Erik Blomberg; 'Gerontion' and 'Whispers of Immortality', translated by Ekelöf; *The Waste Land*, translated by Karin Boye and Erik Mesterton; *Ash-Wednesday*, translated by Erik Lindegren; *Marina*, translated by Erik Blomberg; *Triumphal March*, translated by Johannes Edfelt; two Choruses from *Murder in the Cathedral*, one translated by Anders Osterling, the other by Erik Lindegren and Karl Vennberg; *Burnt Norton*, translated by Artur Lundkvist; and *East Coker*, translated by Gunnar Ekelöf.

D240. . . . Idén om ett Kristet Samhälle . . . Stockholm, Hugo Gebers Förlag [1947]. 92 pp. 19½ cm. (Levande Debatt). 3 kr. A translation, by John Erik Elmberg, of *The Idea of a Christian Society*.

# D. *Translations into Foreign Languages*

D241. . . . Efter Främmande Gudar: Elementarbok i Modernt Kätteri
. . . Stockholm, Norlin Förlag [1947]. 85 pp., 1 blank leaf.
18½ cm. 5 kr. A translation, by Ingvar Högman, of *After
Strange Gods*.

D242. SLÄKTMÖTET . . . Stockholm, Albert Bonniers Förlag [1948].
133, [1] pp., 1 blank leaf. 19½ cm. (Panache Serien). 6.50 kr.
A translation, by Caleb J. Anderson and Karl Vennberg, of
*The Family Reunion*.

D243. . . . Vad är en Klassiker? och Andra Essayer; valda av Lennart
Göthberg . . . [Stockholm] Norlin [1948]. 230 pp., 1 leaf. 20
cm. 11 kr. Contains translations, by Daniel Andreae, of *What
is a Classic?*, *Dante*, 'Religion and Literature', 'William Blake',
'The Humanism of Irving Babbitt', 'Second Thoughts about
Humanism', 'The *Pensées* of Pascal', 'Tradition and the Indivi-
dual Talent', 'The Function of Criticism', 'Baudelaire', and
'The Metaphysical Poets'.

D244. . . . FYRA KVARTETTER . . . Stockholm, Albert Bonniers Förlag
[1948]. 80, [1] pp., 1 blank leaf. 22½ cm. 5.75 kr. Translated by
Artur Lundkvist, Gunnar Ekelöf, and Th. Warburton, with
an Introduction by Warburton.

D245. . . . DE KNEPIGA KATTERNAS BOK . . . [Stockholm] Bonniers
[1949]. 63, [1] pp., incl. illus., 3 col. plates. 22 cm. 8.50 kr. A
translation, by Britt G. Hallqvist, of *Old Possum's Book of
Practical Cats*, with Nicolas Bentley's illustrations.

D246. . . . COCKTAILPARTYT . . . SWEENEY AGONISTES . . . Stockholm,
Albert Bonniers Förlag [1950]. 215, [1] pp. 20½ cm. 10 kr.
Translations of *The Cocktail Party* by Erik Lindegren, and of
*Sweeney Agonistes* by Lindegren and Erik Mesterton.

ANTHOLOGY:

D247. FÖR TRÄDETS SKULL; DIKTER av Karin Boye. Stockholm, A.
Bonnier [1935]. Contains Karin Boye's translation of *The Waste
Land*, pp. 88–124.

PERIODICALS:

D248. TVÅ DIKTER. *Ord och Bild*, XLVI (1937) 164. Translations, by
Johannes Edfelt, of 'Eyes that last I saw in tears', and 'The
wind sprang up at four o'clock'.

D249. EAST COKER. *Bonniers Litterära Magasin*, X. 6 (July/Aug. 1941),
423–8. Translated by Gunnar Ekelöf.

D250. J. ALFRED PRUFROCKS KARLEKSSANG. *BLM*, XI. 4 (Apr. 1942)
255–9. A translation, by Gunnar Ekelöf, of 'The Love Song of
J. Alfred Prufrock'.

# D. *Translations into Foreign Languages*

D251. THE DRY SALVAGES. *BLM*, XIV. 2 (Feb. 1945) 103–9. Translated by Th. Warburton.

D252. LITTLE GIDDING. *1945.* 1 (1945) 16–24. Translated by Th. Warburton.

D253. RAPSODI EN BLÅSIG NATT. *Ord och Bild*, LIV. 9 (1945) 407–8. A translation, by Gunnar Ekelöf, of 'Rhapsody on a Windy Night'.

D254. Författaren och Europas Framtid. *BLM*, XV. 1 (Jan. 1946) 23–28. A translation, by Sonja Bergvall, of 'The Man of Letters and the Future of Europe'.

D255. En Skalds Tankar om den Europeiska Kulturen. *BLM*, XV. 8 (Oct. 1946) 651–8. A translation, by Nils Holmberg, of 'Reflections on the Unity of European Culture'.

D256. SWEENEY AGONISTES. *Prisma*, 5 (1948) 4–15. Translated by Erik Lindegren and Erik Mesterton.

D257. Sagt av Eliot. *Prisma*, 5 (1948) 18–24. Eight selections from essays, chosen and translated by Lindegren and Mesterton.

D258. Strindbergs Inflytande på T. S. Eliot Betydande. *Svenska Dagbladet* (Jan. 20, 1949) 7. A translation of T. S. Eliot's address at the Strindberg Centenary Meeting of the Anglo-Swedish Society in London, January 6, 1949.

D259. Nobelprisets Innebörd, tal vid Nobelfesten på Stockholms Stadshus den 10 December 1948. *BLM*, XVIII. 2 (Feb. 1949) 112–13. A translation of T. S. Eliot's speech of acceptance of the Nobel Prize for Literature.

D260. ANIMULA. *Ord och Bild*, LX. 1 (1951) 12. Translated by Teddy Brunius and Göran B. Johansson.

D261. Huckleberry Finn. *BLM*. XX. 10 (Dec. 1951) 751–6. A translation, by Sven Barthel, of the introduction to the Cresset Library edition of *The Adventures of Huckleberry Finn* (see B 79).

# WELSH

BOOK:

D262. LLADD WRTH YR ALLOR. . . . Llandebie, Llyfrau'r Dryw, Sir Gaerfyrddin [1949]. 71 pp. 19 cm. A translation, by Thomas Parry, of *Murder in the Cathedral*.

# E

---

## APPENDIX:
## MISCELLANEA

# E. *Appendix*: *Miscellanea*

## E1. SYLLABUSES

Between 1916 and 1918, T. S. Eliot gave Extension Courses at Oxford and the University of London, and lectured under the auspices of the London County Council. The Syllabuses of these lectures were printed with his annotations, and copies of those described below may be found in the Houghton Library at Harvard.

*a.* Oxford University Extension Lectures. Syllabus of a Course of six Lectures on Modern French Literature by T. Stearns Eliot, M.A. (Harvard). Oxford, Frederick Hall, Printer to the University . . . 1916

> 6, [5], [2] pp. $18\frac{1}{2} \times 12\frac{1}{2}$ cm. Unbound; sewn.
> Contains a list of recommended books and short descriptions of the six lectures.

*b.* University of London. Syllabus for a Tutorial Class in Modern English Literature by T. S. Eliot, M.A. This Tutorial Class is under the University of London Joint Committee for the Promotion of the Higher Education of Working People. London: University of London Press, 1916.

> 7, [1] pp. $18\frac{1}{2} \times 12\frac{1}{2}$ cm. Unbound; stapled.
> Lists sixteen lectures, with recommended supplementary reading.

*c.* London County Council. Evening Lectures on English Literature. The County Secondary School, High Street, Sydenham, S.E.26. A Course of twenty-five Lectures on Victorian Literature will be delivered at the above-named school on Friday evenings, from 7 to 9 o'clock, beginning on 28th September, 1917. Lecturer . . . T. G[*sic*]. Eliot. For Syllabus of Lectures, see other side.

> [2] pp. $18\frac{1}{2} \times 12\frac{1}{2}$ cm.
> Page 2 lists the titles of the twenty-five lectures.

*d.* [Same as *b*, above, except that the date is 1918].

> 8 pp. $18\frac{1}{2} \times 12\frac{1}{2}$ cm. Unbound; stapled.
> Although the title describes the class as one in Modern English Literature, the lectures actually enumerated are eighteen in Elizabethan Literature, with a reading list.

## E2. OTHER LEAFLETS AND BROADSIDES

*a.* . . . Samuel Taylor Coleridge. 1772–1834 . . . Bradford, Eng., Printed by B. Matthews [1934]

> Post-card. $9 \times 14$ cm. 3*d*. (National Portrait Gallery 192).
> This brief biography of Coleridge was written to accompany the

post-card reproduction, in black and white, of the portrait of Coleridge by Peter Vandyke (1795) which appears on the verso. The card is one of a series of such reproductions sold to visitors at the Gallery, and was published in May 1934. Later printings add '(Photo Printers)' after the name of the printer in the imprint.

b. Lines Written by T. S. Eliot to Accompany this Exhibition of Photographs . . . [London? Printed for H.M. Government] 1940

Broadside. 76½ × 51½ cm. Not for sale.

About fifty copies were printed at a hand-press for posting in the exhibition of British war photographs arranged by E. McKnight Kauffer for the British Pavilion at the New York World's Fair in 1940. The text was reprinted in the United States as 'Defense of the Islands' in *Britain at War, edited by Monroe Wheeler. Text by T. S. Eliot, Herbert Read, E. J. Carter and Carlos Dyer* (New York, The Museum of Modern Art [1941]), p. 8, which was published in an edition of 10,000 copies on May 22, 1941.

c. Language Study Leaflet No. 107 Record Nos. C 3598–603 Four Quartets by T. S. Eliot "His Master's Voice" Recording made under the Auspices of The British Council Author's Note . . . Hayes, Middx., The Gramophone Co. Ltd. [1947]

Broadside. 19 × 13½ cm. Issued only with the records; not sold separately.

The first printing of five hundred copies, issued in September 1947, bears the publication number 'H.2540/947'. Later printings with numbers 'H 2540/1247' (December 1947) and 'H.2540/6/48' (June 1948) have been noted.

d. James Joyce 1882–1941 I C A [Exhibition, June 4–July 12, 1950. London, Printed by Downtons Limited, 1950]

Broadside. illus.(ports.) 102 × 75 cm., folded three times to show above title, 25½ × 37 cm.

This 'catalogue', issued in June 1950, for the Joyce exhibition at the Institute of Contemporary Arts, contains 'The Approach to James Joyce', by T. S. Eliot. The prefatory note to the La Hune Joyce catalogue is also reprinted.

## E3. FOREIGN EDITIONS

a. *Austrian:*

. . . Selected Poems . . . [Vienna] Published for The British Publishers Guild by I.S.B. Political Division A.C.A.(B.E.)[1946]

150 pp., 1 leaf. 18½ cm. (Guild Books No. A 9.) 3 sch.

Contents identical with *Collected Poems 1909–1935*, except that the following poems are omitted: 'Hysteria', 'Conversation

Galante', 'Le Directeur', 'Mélange Adultère de Tout', 'Lune de Miel', 'Dans le Restaurant', Ariel Poems, Minor Poems, 'Burnt Norton'.

*b. Dutch:*

. . . Murder in the Cathedral; with an Introduction and Annotations by Dr. G. Storms. Bussum, P. Brand [1951]

88 pp. 17 cm. (Paul Brand's English Books. Yellow Series No. 1.) 'Notes', 7 pp. laid in at end.

*c. German:*

(1) American Poets: an Anthology of Contemporary Verse, by Leonora Speyer. München, Kurt Wolff Verlag [1923]

132, [1] pp. 25 cm.
Contains 'Portrait of a Lady', by T. S. Eliot, p. 41–45.

(2) . . . Murder in the Cathedral; bearbeitet von Dr. Paul Wenzel. Braunschweig, Berlin, Hamburg, Georg Westermann Verlag, 1949

120 pp., 2 leaves. 14½ cm.
The English text, with notes in German.

(3) . . . What is a Classic? Tradition and the Individual Talent. Kiel, Lipsius & Tischer [1950].

60 p. 21 cm.
The English text, with notes in German.

*d. Japanese:*

(1) Essays . . . With Introduction and Notes by Kazumi Yano . . . Tokyo, Kenkyusha [1935]

6 leaves, liii, 424 pp., 1 leaf. 27 cm. front.(port.) (Kenkyusha English Texts, 4) Reprinted, 1951, as No. CCXV in Kenkyusha British and American Classics.

(2) . . . The Waste Land and Other Poems . . . With Introduction and Notes by T. Kitamura. Tokyo, Kenkyusha [1940]

xi pp., 1 leaf, 144 p., 1 blank leaf. 17½ cm. (Kenkyusha Pocket English Series, 71) 50 yen.
*Contents*: The Waste Land—The Hollow Men—The Love Song of J. Alfred Prufrock—Gerontion—Notes (pp. [63]–144).

*(3) Religion and Literature & Other Essays.

This title is listed as No. 68 of 'Kenkyusha Pocket English Series'.

*e. Swedish:*

(1) Murder in the Cathedral . . . Stockholm, London, The Continental Book Company AB [1945]

2 leaves, 7–87, [1] pp., 1 blank leaf. 18½ cm. (Zephyr Books, a Library of British and American Authors, 85).

'This edition must not be introduced into the British Empire or the U.S.A.'

(2) Twelve Modern Poets: An Anthology edited by Artur Lundkvist . . . Stockholm, London, The Continental Book Company AB [1946]

1 blank leaf, xiii, 220, [2] pp., 1 blank leaf. 18½ cm. (Zephyr Books, 100)

Contains 'Preludes', 'Portrait of a Lady', 'Gerontion', 'Burbank with a Baedeker: Bleistein with a Cigar', 'The Hippopotamus', 'Ash-Wednesday', 'Marina', 'Usk', 'Rannoch, by Glencoe', 'Little Gidding', by T. S. Eliot, pp. [1]–35. Slip relating to 'Little Gidding' tipped in before p. [ix].

## E4. RECORDINGS

A number of recordings of readings by T. S. Eliot have been made. Those listed below were made available to the general public.

*a.* Harvard: 1934: The Hollow Men SS–5052.
                       Gerontion SS–5053.

*b.* Harvard: 1948: The Love Song of J. Alfred Prufrock P.1200–1.

*c.* Harvard: 1947: Journey of the Magi P.1202.
                       A Song for Simeon P.1203.

*d.* Harvard: 1948: Triumphal March P.1204.
                       Difficulties of a Statesman P.1205.

*e.* Harvard: 1947: Fragment of an Agon P.1206–7.

*Note*: All the above Harvard recordings were made available in 1951 on a single long-playing (33½ r.p.m.) record.

*f.* H. M. V.: 1947: Four Quartets C.3598–3603 (6 records).

*g.* Library of Congress, U.S.A.: 1949:
        The Waste Land P.11–13 (3 records).

*h.* Library of Congress, U.S.A.: 1949:
        Ash-Wednesday P.14–15A (1½ records).
        Landscapes: I. New Hampshire. II. Virginia.
        Sweeney Among the Nightingales P.15B (½ record).

# INDEX OF
# TITLES

# INDEX OF TITLES

# Index of Titles

# Index of Titles

# Index of Titles

# Index of Titles

# Index of Titles

# INDEX OF
# NAMES

# INDEX OF NAMES

## (PERSONS, PUBLISHERS, ETC.)

# Index of Names

Descartes, R., C269
De Silva, F., D151
Deustua, R., D229
D'Hangest, G., C149
Dickens, C., B10; C220
Dickinson, G. L., C276
Dobrée, B., B38
Dodge, B36
Donne, J., B23; C101, 139, 167, 291, 304–5; D47
Dos Passos, J., B63
Dostoievsky, F. M., C522
Doubleday, Doran, A7, 12b; B57
Doughty, C. M., C23
Douglas, C382
Downtons, B76
Dowson, E., C374
Doyle, A. C., C283
Dreyer, D192
Drummond, P., D200–1
Dryden, J., A7, 23, 25; B11, 28; C123, 308–9, 317–19, 492
Dudgeon, P. O., D218
Duell, Sloan and Pearce, B56
Duke University Press, B60
Duleba, W., D199
Dupee, F. W., B57
Dutton, E. P., B21
Dyer, C., E2b

Eason, T. W., B74
Edfelt, J., D239, 248
Editions Universitaires, D33
Editorial Hispanica, D210
Editorial Nascimento, D216
Editorial Nova, D218
Edizioni Italiane, D141
Egoist Ltd., A1
Einstein, A., C311
Ekelöf, G., D239, 244, 249–50
Eliot, C., B8
Eliot, T. G., A57a
Elizabeth, Queen, C273; B47
Ellis-Fermor, U. M., C201
Elmberg, J. E., D240
Elton, O., C169
Emecé, D209, 213, 215
Emmanouel, K., D135
Empson, W., D181
English Association, A20; B35; C169
Epesa, D214
Erskine, J., C74

Espasa-Calpe, D208
Espiga, D212
Essex, Earl of, C273
Etchells, F., B11, 20
Euripides, C108

Faber, G., B46; C66
Faber & Faber, A13–14, 15a, b, 16a, b, c, 17–19, 21a, b, e, 23, 24a, 25a, 26a, 27, 29b, c, d, e, 31a, 32a, 33a, 34a, c, 35a, 36c, 37–39, 42, 44b, 45, 51a, 55a, 57b; B32b, 33, 39b, 40, 48, 50–51, 53–54, 62, 64, 66, 78, 81, 84; C520; D4
Faber & Gwyer, A8a, b, 9a, b, 11, 12a; B12–13, 14a, b
Failli, D141
Farjeon, E., C66
Farrar & Rinehart, B16, 26
Farrell, J. T., B67
Fawcett, E. D., C65
Feist, H., D97, 106
Felipe, L., D207, 220
Fenollosa, E., C46
Feo, J. R., D226
Fernandez, R., C184, 230, 299; D46
Film Traders Ltd., B86
Fitzgerald, F. S. K., B63
Fletcher, J., C187
Flint, F. S., B27; C107
Flores, A., D23, 206–7, 216
Fluchère, H., D32, 36, 39, 58, 80–81, 84, 86
Foà, L., D148
Foerster, N., B16; C275
Ford, F. M., B26; C151
Ford, J., C235
Forster, E. M., B76
Forty-five Churches Fund, A26
Fountain Press, A15a
Fowler, H. W., C194
Fox Club, B70
Frazer, J., C153
Frédérik, A., D33
Freud, S., C272
Friedenthal, R., D107
Friedlander, J., B72
Fukase, M., D186
Fukuda, T., D185
Furreg, H., D92
Fussi, B73; D149

Galleon Press, Croydon, A54

# Index of Names

Galleon Press, New York, A14*a*, 19*a*
Gangulee, N., B48, 84
García, J. E., D231
Gardner, C., C105
Gardner, P., C205
Garnett, E., C53
Gaskell, E. C., C345
Gaxotte, P., C271
Geach, E. F. A., C66
Gerber, H., D240
Germain, A., D42
Gescher, L., D130*a*
Gide, A., D64
Gideon-Welcker, C., D96*a*
Giglio, T., D144, 164
Gilbert, S., B67
Girri, A., D218
Givens, S., B67
Göthberg, L., D243
Goethe, J. W. von, C276
Goll, Y., D62
Gosse, E., C91, 103
Gotham Book Mart, A6*a*
Goulden, H. J., A29*a*
Goyert, G., D96*a*
Gramophone Co., E2*c*
Granville-Barker, H., B28
Green, A. K., C283
Gregory, E. C., B46
Grierson, H., B43
Grimble, C. J., C52
Guanda, C142-3
Guidacci, M., D172
Gutner, M., D205
Gyldendal, B69; D191

Habel, C., A46; D89
Hagerup, H., D16
Hall, D., B82
Hall, J., B75
Hallqvist, B. G., D245
Hamilton, R., B74
Hansen, K. H., D122, 128-9
Harcourt, Brace, A8*c*, 16*d*, *e*, 21*c*, *d*, 25*b*, 26*b*, 29*f*, *g*, 31*b*, 32*b*, 33*b*, 34*b*, 35*b*, 44*a*, 51*b*, 52*a*, 55*b*; B5, 30, 39, 80
Harper & Brothers, B41, 55
Harrap, G. G., B58
Harris, C., C412
Harris, J. H., C216
Harrison, G. B., B28

Harvard Printing Office, A47
Harvard University Press, A24*b*, 57; B23
Haskins, C. H., C221
Hasselbalch, S., D13, 17
Haukova, J., D5, 10
Hawkins, D., C460
Hawthorne, N., C67
Hayward, J., A38, 56; B46; C523; D34, 37
Hearnshaw, F. J. C., C186
Helms, Dr., D125
Hemingway, E., B26
Henderson, A. C., A17*a*
Hendry, I., B67
Hendry, J. F., B67
Hennecke, H., A46; D94, 101
Hensel, G., D93, 124
Herbert, G., C305, 329, 434
Herford, C. H., C216, 260
Hermes, G., A14
Heywood, T., C188, 324
Hiller, L., A46; D89
H.M. Stationery Office, B58
Hobbes, T., C186
Hobson, J. A., C214
Hodder and Stoughton, B47
Hodges, C464
Hodgson, R., C339
Högman, I., D241
Hofer, P., A47
Hoffman, F. J., B67
Hogarth Press, A3, 6*c*, 7
Holland, B., C244
Holliday, T. & E., A22
Holloway, E., C191
Holmberg, N., D255
Hood, C. M., C177
Hooker, R., C186, 288
Horton, W. M., B40
Houghton Library, E1
Housman, A. E., C233, 348
Howard, M. S., C20
Hügel, F. von, C244
Hune, La, B72; D41
Huneker, J., C13
Huxley, A., C107, 458
Hyde, L., C320

Ichnowskiej, T., D198
Ikaros, D133
Imprimerie Royale, B77

[ 172 ]

# Index of Names

# Index of Names

# Index of Names

Trent, W. P., C74
Trilling, L., C499
Trotter, W. F., B21
Troy, W., B67
Trundlett, H. B., C52
Turbervile, G., C277
Turgenev, I., C53
Twayne, B82
Tyler, P., A14*a*, 19*a*

Unwin, J. D., C458
Usigli, R., D207

Vail, L., B24
Valéry, P., A52; B6, 65; C109, 523, 539; D39, 51
Van Doren, C., C74
Vandyke, P., E2*a*
Vanecek, A., D6–8
Vanguard Press, B67
Van Oorschot, G. A., D20
Vassar Experimental Theatre, B56
Vaughan, H., C225, 307
Vendryes, J., C194
Vennberg, K., D238–9, 242
Vergil, C566
Victoria, Queen, D211
Vidler, A. R., C464
Vilarino, I., D235
Viljanen, L., D30
Virgil Society, A45; C495
Virginia, University of, A4*a*, 25
Vivante, L., B78
Voeten, B., D22, 25
Vogel, J., D69

Wadsworth, E. A., A4*a*
Wahl, J., D59–61
Walker, H., C166
Wallace, D. E. A., C66
Walpole, H., B26; C469
Wanley, N., C169
Warburton, T., D244, 251–2
Ward, C250, 256
Wardle, M., B6
Waugh, A., C66
Webb, C. C. J., C26

Webster, J., C104, 257, 475
Weightman, J. G., B61
Wellek, R., D9
Wells, H. G., C205
Wenzel, P., E3*c*(2)
Wescott, G., B63
Westermann, D14; E3*c*(2)
Westminster Press, B18
Wharton, E., B63
Wheeler, M., E2*b*
Whibley, C., A20; B9; C76, 102, 171, 266
Whistler, R., A13*a*
Whitehill, J., C345
Whitman, W., C191, 210
Whittet & Shepperson, A48
Williams, C., B68; C510, 521
Wilson, E., B57, 63, 67
Wilson, F. P., C178
Wingate, A., B57
Wise, T. J., C91, 103
Wivel, D15
Wölcken, F., D102
Wolf, A., C24, 202
Wolfe, T., B63
Wolff, W., D104
Woolf, L. & V., A3, 6*c*, 7; C468
Wordsworth, W., A24
World Publishing Co., B63
Wulf, M. de, C189
Wulfsberg, F., D188
Wundt, W., C38
Wydenbruck, N., D90, 95, 121
Wyndham, G., C76

Xydes, A., D136

Yamoto, T., D182
Yeats, J. B., C43
Yeats, W. B., B75; C85, 389, 457
Yeh, K. C., D2

Zabel, M. D., B41
Zacharopoulos, A., D134
Zo-shin-sha, D184
Zukovsky, L., A17*a*